D1472518

New Migrants in the Marketplace

New Migrants
in the
Marketplace:
Boston's Ethnic
Entrepreneurs

Edited by Marilyn Halter

Foreword by Peter L. Berger

UNIVERSITY OF MASSACHUSETTS PRESS / AMHERST

This book is published with the support and cooperation
of the Institute for the Study of Economic Culture
at Boston University and the University of Massachusetts Boston.

Library of Congress Cataloging-in-Publication Data

New migrants in the marketplace : Boston's ethnic
  entrepreneurs / edited by Marilyn Halter ; foreword
  by Peter L. Berger.
        p.   cm.
    Includes bibliographical references and index.
    ISBN 0-87023-963-5 (alk. paper)
    1. Minority business enterprises—Massachusetts—
Boston. 2. Minorities—Employment—
Massachusetts—Boston. 3. Minorities—
Massachusetts—Boston—Economic conditions.
4. Boston (Mass.)—Ethnic relations.   I. Halter,
Marilyn.
HD2346.U5N38   1995
332.6′422′0974461—dc20   94-24122
                                              CIP

British Library Cataloguing in Publication data are available.

Contents

Contents

Foreword

Greater Boston contains what is probably the world's largest concentration of academic and research institutions. It is in these institutions—universities, laboratories, research hospitals—that essential components for a high-technology future are being invented and developed. It is a heady environment, rather intimidating to anyone not versed in the scientific disciplines. Only a short drive or even walk from these centers of futuristic fantasy one can find oneself in an altogether different world, which carries associations with America's past rather than its future. Here are typically grimy streets and rather dilapidated buildings. They are brightened with a multiplicity of small enterprises—restaurants, groceries, beauty parlors, dry cleaning establishments. Most of these enterprises are owned and staffed by recent immigrants, the great majority from the Americas, Asia, and the former Soviet Union. These two worlds of Boston, vastly different though they are from each other, share two important characteristics. Both are cosmopolitan in their ethnic makeup. And both exude an air of great vitality. Is there more of a connection between them? The studies in this volume strongly suggest that there is. Put simply, the vitality of the second feeds the vitality of the first.

The project resulting in this book was sponsored by the Institute for the Study of Economic Culture at Boston University, a research center concerned with the relation between culture and economic behavior. This concern is well expressed throughout this book. It is, of course, possible to study small business (ethnic or otherwise) without reference to cultural and social factors. Economists do this all the time, and it results in important insights. But such study leaves out the gritty reality of the actual lives of people. Only by looking at this reality, which is thoroughly steeped in culture, does one understand the full human significance of the abstract processes traced by the economists. This is the case on any level of the economy. It is especially so with regard to small enterprises that comprise the near-total existence of individuals and families. It may be possible to understand the workings of a large corporation without paying attention to the personal beliefs, values, and lifestyles of its employees. Such thinking is much less plausible if one wants to understand how a mom-and-pop store works.

The value of research in the human sciences does not necessarily lie in the practical significance of its findings. Simple curiosity is enough justification. The rich data reported on in this volume are interesting and frequently fascinating in themselves. They are also of considerable practical importance in at least two areas. It is small business rather than the megacorporation that is the most dynamic generator of jobs in the contemporary American economy. It is of great practical importance, therefore, to understand what makes this type of economic entity tick. Because a strategic portion of small business is occupied by ethnic entrepreneurs, a better understanding of those entrepreneurs is useful indeed. The other area where these findings are relevant, of course, is that of immigration in general. These studies show how ethnic enterprise is not only, in Ivan Light's phrase, a "school for entrepreneurs," but more generally a school for social mobility and also a context of solidarity from which individuals can obtain the confidence to venture out into the wider U.S. society. Put simply, many of the individuals inhabiting the world of high-tech Boston are "graduates" of the other Boston described in this book.

There is a disturbing wave of anti-immigration sentiments in America today, some of it reflecting legitimate concerns, some expressing very ugly cultural and racial prejudices. Whatever the origins of these sentiments, they constitute not only a political but an economic liability. Immigrants continue today, as they have in the past, to be an enormous resource for the vitality of U.S. society and the U.S. economy. The United States is the only major industrial country that has been consistently successful in accepting and integrating immigrants from every part of the world. To be sure, there have been exceptions, problems, and setbacks in this ongoing drama of sociocultural versatility. But these difficulties should not obscure the overall success. The fact becomes especially salient when one compares the United States with its two major competitors in the global economy, Western Europe and Japan. The Europeans are still agonizing over such questions as whether one can be British with a skin color other than white, French with Islamic faith, or German with a Turkish surname. As for Japan, its xenophobia has become a major economic handicap. U.S. openness to immigrants is not only a social and political achievement, but also a comparative advantage in the international game of economic competition. The present volume makes a contribution to our understanding of the vitality that the recent immigrants bring into the life of this society.

Grateful acknowledgment is made for the generous support of this project by the Sarah Scaife Foundation and the Lynde and Harry Bradley Foundation.

Peter L. Berger
Director
Institute for the Study of Economic Culture
Boston University

Acknowledgments

When my best friend growing up, Sandra Krupp, and I both decided to major in American Studies in college, her always sensible father took great delight in teasing us about the likely job prospects with a degree in such an impractical field. "What will you do when you graduate," he would taunt, "open an American Studies store?" Paying no mind to his not-unwarranted skepticism, I not only went on to receive a bachelor's degree in American Studies but pursued a Ph.D. in the subject as well. And while I have yet to actually go into business for myself, I have utilized that American Studies training to research and write about the self-employed. In retrospect, what seemed to be an outlandish proposition turned out to be not so far from the truth. Perhaps my first debt, then, is to Mayer Krupp for his now rather prophetic linkage of the study of culture with the business world as a possible arena for my scholarly pursuits.

More currently and at quite a different level, I am most grateful to Peter L. Berger, founder and director of the Institute for the Study of Economic Culture (ISEC) at Boston University where I have been a research associate since 1990. By formulating the concept of economic culture and then establishing an interdisciplinary center where studies that relate culture to economics can be carried out, he has provided the ideal setting for a project such as this one. Professor Berger has offered his own enthusiastic support and keen guidance on this research from its beginning, while also having assembled a group of scholars at ISEC who together have created an exceptional spirit of collegiality from which I have benefited greatly. I thank the members of our in-house seminar for their regular feedback on this effort, especially Frank Heuberger, Laura Nash, Rob Weller, and Robert Hefner. Funding for this project was generously provided by the Sarah Scaife Foundation and the Lynde and Harry Bradley Foundation.

In the spring of 1992, I convened a conference at ISEC to present this research in progress. In addition to those in attendance whose work is published in this volume, I am indebted to Alejandro Portes, Shelley Tenenbaum, Steve Gold, Birgitte Berger, Silvia Pedraza, Joan Estruch, and Hillel Levine for their participation and thoughtful critical commentaries. Cara Shockley and Paula Kravitz took care of all the conference arrangements. My thanks to Steve Gold for his photographic contribution to this collection and especially for his ongoing friendship. Both Lawrence Fuchs and Sam Bass Warner gave me early advice on the parameters of this study. Their sustained interest in my career has been essential to my development as a scholar. Thanks, also, to Saul Engelbourg for his suggested references.

My investigations into Soviet Jewish entrepreneurship benefited enormously from the research assistance of Pearl Morgovsky. The Haitian component of the study depended on the invaluable assistance of Caroline Hudicourt while Alix and Frantz Cantave helped me launch the Haitian research. I am indebted to Nora Groves of the staff of the Massachusetts Institute for Social and Economic Research for computing the PUMS data and to Jim O'Brien for compiling the index. Working with Paul Wright of the University of Massachusetts Press, who took an early interest in this project, has been a most enjoyable experience.

My final thanks are to my husband, Jonathan, and to my son, Conor, who each have contributed in myriad ways to making our home such a wonderful place to work and play. I am especially appreciative of the idyllic space that Jonathan designed and built for me, the study where much of this book was realized.

Marilyn Halter
May 1994

Chapter 1

Introduction—Boston's Immigrants Revisited: The Economic Culture of Ethnic Enterprise

Marilyn Halter

More than 160 years ago American society reached its zenith in levels of self-employment. During the 1820s and 1830s, great religious upheavals coincided with a wide-ranging flurry of small business activity to create what has been called "a shopkeeper's millennium," particularly in the Northeast (Johnson 1978).[1] As the early nineteenth-century market economy expanded, the proportion of free white Americans owning their own businesses soared to 80 percent (Corey 1966). Since that time entrepreneurship of this type has been in steady decline. However, the growth and significance of *ethnic* entrepreneurialism in recent American socioeconomic life is a phenomenon that has generated much contemporary interest across a broad political and ideological spectrum and among scholars, policymakers, and community activists alike.

Within social scientific scholarship, most had predicted that small businesses in the United States would all but disappear by the late twentieth century; still others projected that the significance of ethnicity in relation to economic success would greatly diminish by this stage of advanced capitalism.[2] Interestingly, the giants of modern sociology, including Marx and Weber, all underestimated the vitality of entrepreneurialism in the modern state, and none have contributed theoretical models that could account for its continued importance.[3] Thus, an unlikely consensus evolved among scholars on the right, left, and center that entrepreneurship would simply become obsolete in advanced economies. Yet the entrepreneurial spirit has shown itself to be surprisingly resilient in a postindustrial economy, particularly in the case of ethnic-based enterprises. The small business owner as folk hero in American culture endures.

Ethnic entrepreneurialism exemplifies an alternative path to socioeconomic adjustment and mobility in America, representing an avenue directly opposite to that which had crystallized in the literature derived from the perceived experience of turn-of-the-century newcomers. Popular views often held that immigrants of the earlier wave succeeded by joining the mainstream as rapidly as possible, by losing their distinctive group characteristics. The strategies exhibited by members of today's ethnic economies, just as in the past, reflect considerable cultural cohesiveness and continuity. The road to successful adaptation and upward mobility depends precisely on *not* assimilating too much. Social resources based on a common cultural identity are maintained as a way to compensate for other disadvantages such as racial discrimination or a lack of sufficient start-up capital. Thus, the recent scholarship documenting the development of successful ethnic enterprise constitutes a formidable challenge to prevailing theories of both immigrant incorporation and the workings of a postindustrial society.

Sociologists studying immigrants who have arrived in the United States since 1965 first drew attention to the sizable number of new immigrants opening and operating small businesses. Wider public awareness of this phenomenon has also spread, often the result, unfortunately, of well-publicized conflicts between foreign-born shopkeepers and their native-born (often minority) customers. At the same time, particularly in the wake of the devastation resulting from the 1992 riots in Los Angeles and in response to the entrenchment of urban poverty in pockets throughout the United States, programs to promote local entrepreneurship are being put forth from a broad range of political perspectives as possible remedies. Proponents of entrepreneurial initiatives come from the private sector as well as from community bases such as black nationalist self-help groups, and federally sponsored programs, such as urban enterprise zones. As incongruous as it may initially appear, even the political left has gotten into the act, as sociologist Steve Gold (1992, 167) pointed out in his study of refugee communities in California. Gold noted that some individuals with a more traditionally collectivist approach to questions of economic success are recognizing the community value of ethnic-based business activity. Local antipoverty agencies now sponsor microenterprise training programs staffed by organizers known as "enterprise agents," and networks of nonprofit grass

2

roots lending programs designed to bolster self-employment are being implemented in low-income communities across the country. The appeal of successful immigrant entrepreneurship as a response to the challenges of a multiracial, multiethnic urban environment can be viewed as compatible with a variety of sociopolitical outlooks.

New immigrants and their ventures have already been credited with revitalizing decaying and depopulated neighborhoods in America's cities and older suburbs, rejuvenating crumbling business districts overrun with vacant storefronts, restoring dilapidated residences, and, through the repopulation process, expanding the tax base of metropolitan areas that have been dying out with the decline of the industrial city and in the aftermath of the failures of urban renewal. In an era of massive layoffs by large firms, small and midsize companies in the 1990s have been shown to be increasingly important in creating employment opportunities. Numerous contemporary analyses demonstrate that small business rather than the large corporation provides most jobs in the United States today and that these enterprises are leading the economy out of recession.[4]

Indeed, since the 1880s, immigrants have been overrepresented in American small business endeavors, and the latest wave of newcomers to our shores are again infusing this sector of the economy with renewed vitality. Since the passage of the landmark Hart-Celler Act of 1965, immigrants, particularly from Asia, Latin America, and the Caribbean, have been streaming into the United States in ever-increasing numbers. Legislation passed in 1990 reinforced the likelihood that the borders of this country will be kept relatively open. Under the 1990 act, legal immigration has averaged about 1 million people a year until 1994 and is unlikely to go below 500,000, even if calls for restriction are heeded. In addition, according to the U.S. Census Bureau, illegal migration to the United States has totaled approximately 300,000 annually in recent years. Immigrants produced roughly 39 percent of the overall U.S. population growth in the 1980s. At this rate, the closing years of the twentieth century will become *the* decade of immigration surpassing even the high-water mark of mass migration reached during the first decade of the century. Currently, the United States and neighboring Canada are the only major industrial societies that have successfully absorbed large numbers of immigrants from just about anywhere in the world—with very few exceptions, which have specific historical explanations.

More than fifty years ago, Oscar Handlin, the father of modern immigration studies, chose Boston as the site for his pioneering investigation of

Table 1. Selected Immigrant / Ethnic Groups in Massachusetts

Place of Birth	Male	%	Female	%	Total
Cambodia	5,373	48.2	5,764	51.8	11,137
Dominican Republic	8,780	45.7	10,432	54.3	19,212
Greece	4,911	55.2	3,980	44.8	8,891
Haiti	8,937	48.2	9,616	51.8	18,553
Jamaica, Trinidad, BWI	4,984	44.4	6,244	55.6	11,228
Puerto Rico	32,596	46.1	38,056	53.9	70,652
USSR	4,811	44.7	5,959	55.3	10,770

Source: 1990 U.S. Census, 5 % Public Use Microdata Sample (PUMS)

immigrant cultures in an urban setting. *Boston's Immigrants,* a community study that broke down the disciplinary boundaries between history and the social sciences, became a model for many social historians. Several decades later, our book takes a new look at Boston's immigrants—this time the focus is on the economic culture and small business activity of several recently arrived populations, including Jews from the former Soviet Union, British West Indians (from Jamaica, Trinidad, Barbados, and Montserrat), Greeks, Puerto Ricans, Dominicans, Khmer (Cambodians), and Haitians. Tables 1 and 2 list total official numbers of migrants from these groups to both Massachusetts and the Boston Metropolitan Area since 1965. In some cases, however, these tabulations represent severe undercounts because of the large undocumented population as well as high rates of internal geographic mobility. Furthermore, the figures are based on foreign place of birth and, therefore, do not include American-born children of recent immigrants, who, in some cases, constitute a considerable proportion of the ethnic community. In the case of the Haitians, it is estimated that illegal residents actually outnumber those of legal standing. Wherever possible, we have also relied on figures quoted by local community leaders and consulate officials who often provide a more accurate picture.[5]

Boston is particularly well suited to a comparative study of this kind because of the diversity of its immigrant populations. Unlike most cities with large concentrations of immigrants, no one ethnic group predominates. Boston's newcomers also come from more widely varied educational and cultural backgrounds. Yet the total immigrant population is

Table 2. Selected Immigrant/Ethnic Groups in the Boston Metropolitan Area

Place of Birth	Male	%	Female	%	Total
Cambodia	1,584	47.4	1,757	52.6	3,341
Dominican Republic	3,805	44.7	4,698	55.3	8,503
Greece	3,085	57.1	2,320	42.9	5,405
Haiti	7,790	47.9	8,466	52.1	16,256
Jamaica, Trinidad, BWI	3,789	45.1	4,607	54.9	8,396
Puerto Rico	10,168	46.7	11,591	53.3	21,759
USSR	3,474	43.9	4,442	56.1	7,916

Source: 1990 U.S. Census, 5 % Public Use Microdata Sample (PUMS)

still relatively small, at least when compared to concentrations in the major cities of New York, California, or Florida. Thus, there is an opportunity for researchers to examine and compare the adaptation of different ethnic groups within an environment that is not overwhelmed by recent arrivals. Moreover, Massachusetts is little studied in the literature on recent immigration and in the scholarship on ethnic enterprise, providing a potentially valuable laboratory for future comparative studies in this field.

In the 1980s, the state of Massachusetts and the Greater Boston Metropolitan Area experienced huge economic growth that drew many newcomers, transforming the demographic makeup of the region. According to 1990 census figures, the commonwealth ranked fifth in the United States in refugee arrivals and seventh in immigrant arrivals, meaning that the population was diversifying faster than most other states in the last ten years. An estimated 245,000 immigrants and refugees made Massachusetts, whose total population is about 6 million, their home in the 1980s. The city of Boston mirrored this pattern of prosperity and diversity, with its foreign-born population increasing to 20 percent of the total while the economy held strong and unemployment fell. For the first time in forty years, Boston had a net growth in population, up by 11,000 from 1980, at a time when many other older cities like it, including Philadelphia, Baltimore and Chicago, lost population. In the community of Chelsea, adjacent to Boston proper, 70 percent of public schoolchildren live in families where English is not the first language.

The sustained expansion of the 1980s drew people from both the high and low ends of the economic scale. The region's banking, financial, and real estate sectors flourished, requiring a well-educated labor force. Because growth was experienced throughout the economy, unskilled workers could also find employment in low-paying jobs shunned by others. In addition to purely economic incentives, Massachusetts has been the first choice for significant numbers of political refugees. In addition to its purely economic incentives, Massachusetts has been the first choice for significant numbers of political refugees. It also has seen a net gain in secondary refugee settlement every year since the Refugee Act became law in 1980. The commonwelath has a long history of providing refuge to individuals seeking freedom from religious and political persecution and continues to represent that tradition well.

The recent influx has not only changed the face of older ethnic neighborhoods but also reshaped the composition of the Hispanic and Asian communities of Greater Boston. In 1980, Puerto Ricans represented the majority of the city's Hispanic population at 54 percent; by 1990 that number had decreased to 42 percent. The balance is made up of Mexicans and Cubans (7 percent) and what the U.S. Census Bureau designates "other Hispanics," a catchall term that is largely made up of Dominican arrivals. Similarly, the commonwealth's Asian population has diversified in the last decade. Chinese are no longer the majority statewide. In Boston, three of every four Asians were Chinese in 1980, whereas by 1990 the ratio was down to three in five. An increase in the proportion of Vietnamese newcomers, a population that almost quadrupled in size, has much to do with this shift.[6]

Although the flow of new immigrants to the region continues strong into the 1990s, the boom in the economy has not been similarly sustained. Since about 1988, Massachusetts has experienced a recession, the worst slump since the Second World War. The defense and computer industries were hard hit, and the banks became overextended. A 1993 study listed the state, once a mecca for entrepreneurs, as thirty-third in the nation for business start-ups (Birch et al. 1993). More long-standing residents and enterprises have moved away from the commonwealth, seeking greater opportunity in the southern and western states. Some people and jobs are relocating to areas with milder weather, but the new immigrants streaming into the state have the potential to take their places and to warm the entrepreneurial climate in the region.

This comparative research into Boston's ethnic entrepreneurs addresses the question of what accounts for variations in self-employment patterns among national-origin groups. The populations in this study show widely differing rates of self-employment and levels of poverty (see tables 3 and 4). Related objectives are to determine what is distinctively ethnic about the immigrant business and whether these distinctive cultural features contribute to the success of the enterprise. Ethnicity as a factor of economic life can be expressed in many different forms, such as the marketing of ethnic products, employment of coethnics, relationship to coethnic customers, cultural capital generated through ethnic-based resources, and strategies of capitalization. In general, ethnic enterprise studies have found ethnicity to be a highly viable and enduring element of modern societies. They emphasize immigrant cooperation to show that traditional and modern forms of behavior can be mixed to produce a potent economic brew for ethnic entrepreneurs.

In his final chapter in a collection of essays on immigrant entrepreneurs in Britain, Richard Jenkins presents an overview with suggestions for further research. Paramount on his agenda is the need for more *qualitative* studies. According to Jenkins the possibilities for enhancing this field of scholarship, as well as the ability to more sharply analyze the distinctions between structural and cultural elements, rest with a greater emphasis on comparative research that is firmly rooted in localized in-depth case studies. Such an approach, he argues, is the optimal vehicle for determining how decisions are made and actions taken. Although not claiming outright that ethnography is the only or best way to accomplish these objectives, he strongly hints at the significance of anthropological perspectives for garnering the detailed empirical data required to develop convincing cultural models of interpretation. Jenkins also advises that these microlevel studies be situated in the inner cities as the most desirable venue for broadening the scope of research related to ethnic business development (Ward and Jenkins 1984, 231–38).

The design of the Boston immigrant entrepreneurs project contains all the research dimensions that Jenkins prescribed as crucial to bettering our understanding of the phenomenon of ethnic enterprise. Using an ethnographic approach, the study is comparative, urban, and oriented toward an exploration of cultural variables. Moreover, this inquiry adds another ingredient to the recipe for sound qualitative research: a historical perspective on the contemporary problem under consideration. Wherever possible, we have attempted to reconstruct the entrepreneurial milieu of the premigration culture and to trace the development of small businesses among earlier generations of coethnics, when such economies existed in Boston. The Greeks and Russian Jews, for example, have had a significant presence in the Boston metropolis since the late nineteenth century; the British West Indian and Puerto Rican communities date back to the period between the two World Wars. The Dominican, Khmer, and Haitian populations, however, are arriving in large numbers for the first time with this most recent migration. Particularly in the case of the Greeks, the existence of an already well-established coethnic economy serves to enhance the possibilities of success for the newest wave of immigrants interested in going into business for themselves.

The bulk of this volume consists of essays based on the empirical research conducted in Boston and devoted to each immigrant population under study. However, Ivan Light, one of the leading scholars in the field of ethnic enterprise studies, adds a most welcome theoretical contribution to the book that serves to refine and more sharply define critical concepts and terminology, at the same time stretching the horizon of inquiry related to this timely topic. Light is concerned about the lack of clarity, or as he has termed it the "conceptual anarchy," of this subject and seeks especially to reframe the parameters of the two most frequently employed concepts in the literature—the ethnic economy and the ethnic enclave economy. These two ideas are typically used as if they were synonymous, but Light presents a convincing challenge to this approach, arguing that the two notions are clearly not the same and demonstrating, furthermore, that they derive from differing research traditions. He proposes a new theoretical perspective that replaces the centrality of the ethnic enclave economy with the broader umbrella concept of the ethnic economy.

This collection is organized to give the reader both overview and particulars, with Light's theoretical and historiographical essay framing the local, empirically based chapters and suggesting the broader implications of the Boston research. For example, in arguing for the use of other criteria in addition to the standard measure of relative wage differentials as indicators of the success of an ethnic economy, Light points out that such economies have served as training grounds for entrepreneurship, and, therefore, gains may not necessarily be realized solely in monetary terms. Studies have demonstrated that those who are employed in the ethnic economy are more likely than others to become self-employed themselves.[7] In this sense, Light refers to the ethnic economy as a "school for entrepreneurs."

The results of several of the Boston case studies included in this volume strongly reinforce his argument that the value of ethnic entrepreneurship can be assessed in broader terms than comparative short-term earnings. Instead, these kinds of formations can have a multiplier effect. Indications of the significance of the role of an ethnic enterprise as a school for future entrepreneurs were consistently noted in the research. This does not necessarily translate into a simple one-to-one correspondence where all employees in an ethnic business later become owners themselves or where every child of an entrepreneur grows up to take over the family business, although certainly there were numerous examples of both such correlations.

The point to be made is that, overall, the ethnic economy provides a platform both for its coethnic employees and for the second generation to enter the mainstream in positions of advantage, whether they actually go into business or not. For instance, among the Greeks, the pattern of newly arrived immigrants seeking employment in a coethnic establishment, learning the workings of the enterprise, and then going into business for themselves is quite characteristic of the Boston population. A concurrent tendency among the children of Greek entrepreneurs, as well as of Soviet Jews, Khmer, Haitians, and British West Indians is for them to seek professional occupations rather than to follow in their parents' footsteps and maintain the family business. But the economic and social resources resulting from the successful family business are what enables the immigrant children to attain higher levels of education and go on to obtain professional jobs.

Moreover, patterns of entrepreneurship may vary with succeeding generations. For example, the Jews of today are no longer enterprising in the same way that they were at the turn of the century when they were starting small businesses in such large numbers, but a high rate of self-employment still exists. Today, proportionately larger numbers are employed for themselves as independent professionals, particularly as doctors and lawyers. When the child of the owner of a Russian Jewish deli grows up to become a physician, a certain vitality has survived that transition, and that force is not simply a cultural survival but also an economic advantage. Such efforts still lead to an economic basis of ethnic solidarity, but the definition of self-employment has shifted over time.

Each course outlined above represents a different avenue of upward mobility. But all stem from the initial exposure to the ethnic economy, and all bring returns both to the individuals themselves and to the general wealth of the ethnic community. This multiplier effect has historical precedents, as has been demonstrated for the Jewish and Japanese paths of mobility, two minority groups that are among the most successful in America. The historical and contemporary examples testify to the efficacy of Light's assertion that the ethnic economy be viewed as a springboard to future rewards, both economic and social, and not just in terms of immediate relative earnings in comparison with the general labor market.

It is the *interactive* nature of culture and the structure of social relations that forms the theoretical foundation for this project. Scholarship in the field of ethnic enterprise studies has been split into two broad categories—the structuralist approach, emphasizing context of opportunity and situational factors, and the cultural perspective, with its focus on varying ethnic resources and propensities. A review of the historiography would reveal how each of these approaches has been useful in advancing our understanding of the phenomenon of ethnic enterprise in the past. The best work on the subject, however, evidences considerable overlap between the two perspectives. Furthermore, theoretically, the notion of social structure as existing apart from human interpretive processes is simply less sound than formulations that posit a dynamic interaction between contextual and cultural dimensions.

The concern has been raised that, in taking this cultural turn, stereotyping as well as an ethnic or racially prejudiced analysis will result. The incorporation of immigrant value systems within the American context as formulated here is not meant as a throwback to earlier social theory of a culturally deterministic nature nor to historical contributions with a filiopietistic bent. To recognize the influence of differing cultural constructions and ethnic values in the adaptation process is to restore a measure of empowerment to the immigrant as historical actor. Such an approach allows room for researchers to take into account how the immigrant entrepreneurs see themselves, to assess the way in which individuals operate from the actor's viewpoint. Differences in behavior be-

Table 3. Self-Employed by Selected Immigrant/Ethnic Groups

Place of Birth	Massachusetts	% Self-Employed Boston Metropolitan Area
Cambodia	2.3	0.9
Dominican Republic	2.9	2.8
Greece	18.1	13.9
Haiti	1.5	1.3
Jamaica, Trinidad, BWI	1.7	2.3
Puerto Rico	1.6	1.7
USSR	4.0	4.8

Source: 1990 U.S. Census, 5 % Public Use Microdata Sample (PUMS)

tween ethnic groups can be understood in terms of culturally derived choices within these situational limitations.

Are there particular ethnic populations, then, that hold what Peter Berger has called "a comparative cultural advantage" when it comes to entrepreneurial activity? Caesar Mavratsas argues strongly in this volume that in the case of the Greek-Americans, there most definitely does exist an economic ethos promoting values highly compatible with entrepreneurship and that it is precisely this value system—individual autonomy exercised within close family ties, practicality, and a strong work ethic—that explains the disproportionate entrepreneurship of Greek immigrants in this country. The preponderance of Greeks in business locally, as indicated by the high rates of self-employment in the tabulations of selected immigrant groups for this study, supports his claim (see table 3). He describes an emergent hybrid Greek-American culture, estranged from both Greece and America but drawing on elements from both to create a unique form in the United States.

The centrality of the family economy to small business endeavors is borne out by the Greek example, with the traditional gender roles of male ownership and female support services characterizing most of the establishments. With one exception, Soviet Jews, all the populations in the Boston study follow a similar pattern. Typically, the husband is the sole proprietor and the wife works for the business, anywhere from a few hours to full time, performing such tasks as cashier, salesclerk, bookkeeper, cook, or waitress. In some instances of immigrant entrepreneurship, managing the books has become the specific domain of the woman, as preliminary research into gender divisions among Koreans indicates.[8] Women also predominate in the networks of West Indian rotating credit associations in Boston. Men may contribute to the pool, but the bankers are almost always women. Women handling and managing the money in such business-related efforts is clearly acceptable to most, but independent female ownership is still minimal.

Apart from the Soviet Jewish case, women owned only 10 to 15 percent of the businesses in each of the populations studied, and these were characteristically female enterprises, such as beauty shops and child care centers. Most often, these were single women, who were either divorced or widowed. The exception, though limited in scope, is a tendency among non–Chinese Khmer married women to hold primary ownership of traditional female ventures. By contrast, almost half the proprietors of Soviet Jewish businesses, married or not, were female, and the types of goods and services they offered ranged from the usual female establishments such as skin care and nail salons to furniture sales, restaurants, and grocery stores. Like their male counterparts, Russian Jewish women did not have experience with self-employment in the Soviet Union, but they did come from a society where full and equal participation in the work force was expected for both husband and wife, a situation that clearly has been transplanted to their new circumstances in this country.

An interactive model was also the basis for Peggy Levitt's work on the Puerto Rican and Dominican populations in Boston, this time providing the basis to explain their disproportionately *low* rate of self-employment and to conclude that sociocultural resources engender and constrain business development, often simultaneously. Taking her cues from the sentiments and definitions expressed by the owners themselves, she offers a broader interpretation of the meaning of success to Boston's Latino community, highlighting the significant social role played by these ethnic enterprises within it.

Similarly, Haitian entrepreneurship in Boston has, thus far, realized minimal economic success. But the business sector has played a vital social role in the community. Catering to a primarily coethnic clientele, these small, often marginal enterprises are an essential gathering place for sociocultural and political interaction among compatriots, serving as a support network to ease the adaptation process and as a vehicle to sustain Haitian-American cultural identity. A defining element of this social network is the intricate link between the businesses, the nonprofit community service sector, and the extensive Haitian media presence in the Greater Boston area.

Employing an economic culture framework makes possible the identification of various interethnic differences in response to available opportunity structures. Our study is especially interested in the range of ethnic strategies used to deal with the particular external constraints resulting from racial discrimination and consciously examines the factor of race as it interacts with culture in determining entrepreneurial success. Although several historical and sociological schools of thought have had as their central organizing theme a contrast between immigrant adaptation and native black incorporation in many arenas, including rates and success of self-employment, the Boston project explores racial-ethnic differences among immigrant groups. Typically, in theories of racial and ethnic formation, the categories of race and ethnicity are conflated. However, we are primarily concerned with comparing non-white to white immigrants, rather than white immigrants to black natives. The analysis of race becomes even more complex when European, Latin American, Caribbean, and Asian peoples are involved.

The range of populations in our study includes five groups that define themselves or are defined by the wider society as either black or non-white—the British West Indians, Puerto Ricans, Dominicans, Haitians, and Khmer. Though all but the Khmer originate from the Caribbean region, they come with strikingly diverse cultural backgrounds, speaking French, English, and Spanish creoles, practicing various religions, and drawing on different cultural traditions. The ways that racial differences affect their experiences with self-employment in the host society has been a significant issue in this research project.

Recent compilations of the relationship between ethnicity, entrepreneurial status, and personal income reinforce the importance of taking race seriously. The results show wide differences in the average personal earnings of ethnic entrepreneurs, with annual incomes in excess of $40,000 for those of Jewish ancestry to less than $13,000 among Hispanics. What was most significant about these figures was that the average personal earnings of the self-employed from racial-ethnic minority groups never reached as high as $20,000, whereas all the white ethnic groups made at least $21,000 or more (Butler and Herring 1991, 89–90).

Table 4. Poverty Level by Selected Immigrant/Ethnic Groups

Place of Birth	Massachusetts	% below Poverty Level Boston Metropolitan Area
Cambodia	39.2	25.1
Dominican Republic	34.6	37.9
Greece	10.9	10.2
Haiti	19.9	20.6
Jamaica, Trinidad, BWI	17.2	18.0
Puerto Rico	53.0	46.1
USSR	30.3	28.0

Source: 1990 U.S. Census, 5 % Public Use Microdata Sample (PUMS)

These findings are a stark indication of the relationship between race and the realization of economic gains through business participation. Indeed, comparative data based on the Boston sample reinforce these findings, with the two white populations, Greeks and Soviet Jews, showing the highest rates of self-employment. Levels of poverty among these groups, however, do not necessarily correlate with self-employment rankings nor with racial composition (see tables 3 and 4).

To illustrate, Violet Johnson's study of British West Indians begins to debunk a commonly held belief concerning West Indian superiority in the business arena as compared to native-born black Americans. Her findings show that the cultural features of hard work, revolving credit associations, and family economy associated with the West Indian immigrant population have been rechanneled into occupational categories within the service sector and to maintenance of economic stability rather than toward entrepreneurial activity and upward mobility. She argues here that the inability to achieve entrepreneurial success is due to situational factors that have undermined the development of a viable business community among West Indians in Boston.

The portrait she presents exemplifies what John Butler in his recent book, *Entrepreneurship and Self-Help among Black Americans,* has called economic detour, a theory he revives from M. S. Stuart's work on entrepreneurship developed in the 1930s. This concept refers to the ways that enterprising African Americans have been historically stunted in their entrepreneurial growth by being forced to sell in a restricted market. Other middleman minority enterprises, for example Chinese laundries and Japanese restaurants, also faced hostility from the wider society but, nonetheless, were able to take advantage of a broader market. African American business people were not allowed to participate in the larger economy, first because of limitations imposed by legalized segregation policies and later because of similar patterns of de facto segregation that still persist in contemporary urban enclaves (Butler 1991, 71–76).

Contrary to popular belief, Violet Johnson's assessment finds little difference in levels of West Indian and African American business success in Boston. However, she demonstrates that the West Indian values and resources that might have energized the business sector had economic segregation not been a factor are being reoriented toward family maintenance and intensive labor force participation, particularly within the service sector. When compared to white ethnic groups in this study, rather than the traditional comparison with native-born blacks, British West Indians fall far behind in levels of small business activity.

The position of British West Indians is indicative of the complexities involved in any evaluation of the overall success of immigrant incorporation into the economy. Although Light's essay brings clarity to the larger concept of the ethnic economy, some conceptual confusion still exists concerning the specific strategies that ethnic entrepreneurs employ. Differing ethnic populations use a variety of approaches that all function in one way or another through social networks, but as Light has pointed out, not all these strategies make up an ethnic enclave.

The necessary conditions for the development of an enclave require sizable amounts of people, capital, and entrepreneurial expertise. This means that some middleman minority groups simply do not constitute an ethnic enclave. In the case of the British West Indians, a mix of ethnic strategies appears to be at work. Suzanne Model (1993) has coined the term "ethnic niche" to describe places in the actual mainstream economy where for one reason or another a particular ethnic group happens to gain an advantage, such as the historical concentration of Bohemians in cigar making or Jews in the garment industry. West Indians have carved out an ethnic niche for themselves, while simultaneously playing a middleman role vis-à-vis the rest of the black population.

Proportionate to white ethnic groups, British West Indians have not been as successful in business; nonetheless, in their middleman minority position they rank comparatively higher in per capita participation when measured against other Caribbean and Latino populations. At the same time, the niche strategy is evidenced by their having captured a place for themselves in the health care sector, as nurses, nurses' aides, and hospital workers, establishing networks to maintain and expand that entry into the economy. For British West Indians, this combination has worked quite well. Among the groups in the Boston study, they are second only to the Greeks in having the smallest percentage living below the poverty level, well ahead of their Latino counterparts (see table 4). According to the 1990 census report, Jamaicans were ranked highest in median income of any black immigrant group. When evaluating the success, or lack of it, of West Indian entrepreneurship in relation to other groups, one must take into account the larger picture of ethnic insertion into the economy.

Similarly, the Greek immigrants in Massachusetts have found an ethnic niche that is, at the same time, an entrepreneurial niche. Greeks have developed a locus in the economy by the successful operation of restaurants, especially pizza parlors, throughout the Greater Boston area. Yet, spatially, the Greeks do not constitute an ethnic neighborhood as do Boston's Khmer and Latino populations, groups whose businesses are geographically concentrated in coethnic residential areas serving coethnic clientele. Neither do the former Soviet Jewish émigrés exhibit locational aggregation, especially when compared to the earlier settlement of Jewish immigrant businesses in the Boston area where clear-cut ethnic neighborhoods existed.

The recent Jewish arrivals are much more spatially dispersed. Certainly there are greater numbers in the Brookline, Brighton, and North Shore sectors of the metropolis, but these are not cohesive enclaves with businesses serving immediate coethnic neighborhoods. The population is more diffused; the enterprises are more widely scattered. Yet these establishments cannot be said to be completely isolated operations, neither from each other nor from the Soviet Jewish community at large. Russian and Ukrainian Jewish entrepreneurs rely heavily on coethnics for capitalizing their businesses. They employ compatriots, and they maintain a fairly intensive social network. Like the Greeks, they cater, however, to both coethnic and non-coethnic customers.

In terms of economic strategies, this is not the pattern of an ethnic enclave, niche, or neighborhood. In thinking about the Greek and the Soviet Jewish economies, another term may be useful: an ethnic web economy. In such a configuration, a clear pattern of interconnectedness is evidenced, but spatially the clustering is more dispersed and the population more spread out than in an ethnic neighborhood or enclave. Ethnic interdependence is still very much at play, but it functions through a complex web of integral but separated parts, a networking of social and cultural resources, that, when functioning well, constitutes an intricate whole.[9]

The former Soviet Jews are one of two populations in the Boston study that have refugee status. The others are the Khmer settlers. The popular media have speculated that governmental assistance provided for refugees gives them an economic advantage. Our research does not support such a claim. The aid offered is minimal and of short duration. For most, assistance in finding housing and learning the language has not necessarily translated into help with job procurement.[10] However, these two refugee populations do share a common experience in being what can be termed "twice minorities": people who have had previous experience as minorities in another locale before arriving at their current destination.[11]

In the case of the Khmer refugees, Nancy Smith-Hefner demonstrates that the Sino-Khmer population is the most entrepreneurial of the Cambodians in the Greater Boston area. The Chinese were minorities in Cambodia and are still a minority in this country, whereas the "pure Khmer" are having to adjust to their role as a minority group in the United States and, hence, are having more difficulty adapting. Smith-Hefner discusses the overall obstacles to successful business participation among the Khmer as a whole, but she points out that because the Sino-Khmer come to the United States accustomed to operating as a minority group, bringing the flexibility and risk-taking characteristics of disadvantaged populations to their new situation, they hold a slight advantage over the general Khmer population.

Similarly, the recent Russian Jewish refugees have left a situation where they were a disadvantaged group, having experienced generations of European and Soviet anti-Semitism. One of the values learned in this process was that of working for oneself rather than working for others. This strategy, undertaken to circumvent hostile conditions, has been transplanted to their new society. They, also, are twice minorities. Furthermore, like the Khmer, the Russian Jewish population exhibits intragroup differences in relation to entrepreneurial activity. The most business-oriented are those who come from the Ukraine, an area where anti-Semitism was most virulent.

Defying our stereotype of the poor and huddled masses, the most recent influx of newcomers to our shores not only come from widely varying ethnic and racial backgrounds but also are as likely to disembark from a jumbo jet carrying designer luggage as from the steerage of an overcrowded boat with the requisite tattered bundles hoisted over their shoulders. New immigrants are arriving with a range of educational and skill levels unprecedented in the history of migration to this country. Yet even those who enter with extensive professional training face the difficulties of learning the workings of an unfamiliar social environment, especially the challenge of becoming proficient enough in English to successfully communicate their skills. Others find that what they are best trained to do is not needed in their new surroundings. Some come with little or no job skills; others were proprietors of small businesses in the premigration setting and are trying their luck again in the United States. For ethnic minorities in America, whether downwardly mobile upon arrival or starting from the bottom, self-employment is, and has been, one of the more promising routes to upward mobility. Ethnic businesses provide their communities with sources of solidarity and mobility within a hostile environment.

The most recent wave of immigrants have demonstrated, as did earlier generations of newcomers, a willingness to work long hours and to take risks, carving out new markets for goods and services. Dominicans are buying bodegas, often purchased from Puerto Ricans; Haitian taxi drivers own cabs previously driven by Eastern Europeans; and recent Soviet Jewish refugees take over shoe repair businesses from Jewish cobblers who had fled czarist Russia earlier in the century. Some of the recent arrivals, such as the Cambodian manicurist, the Jamaican baker, or the Haitian grocer, are generating new start-up businesses, fulfilling fresh consumer demands that have a favorable impact on overall economic growth. As the twentieth century draws to a close, immigrant entrepreneurs are providing a significant boost to the economy and to the future of this country.

A Note on Methodology

With each ethnic group in this project, the researchers collected data by completing in-depth, open-ended taped interviews with from twenty-five to thirty owners of a variety of small businesses in the Boston area, including the self-employment categories of retail shopkeepers, taxicab drivers, and personal and entertainment services. All of those inter-viewed had migrated to the United States as adults (eighteen years or older). Informal interviews were also done with key nonbusiness eth-nic community respondents. Usually interviews were conducted in the native language of the interviewee, although some were conducted in English when the respondent was comfortable speaking it. Fieldwork also involved participant observation, including attendance at cultural events, church services, family gatherings, and community meetings.

In addition to citing individual examples from the oral accounts to support larger theoretical points and using this material as factual docu-mentation related to the topic at hand, an attempt was made to discern what the interview process itself might reveal about each cultural group, an approach that is in keeping with the hermeneutic method. For exam-ple, the Russian Jewish respondents showed a consistent pattern of in-terest in the research itself and an appreciation of the value of academic scholarship. Often they would offer unsolicited analysis of the scholarly content of the research and understood that intellectual inquiry could be an end in itself. Several people who were contacted directly or heard about the study secondhand took the initiative (in decidedly entrepre-neurial fashion) to send me résumés with the hope that they could be hired as research assistants or translators on the project. This con-trasted sharply to the response of other groups in our study, where no such analytic input was forthcoming and where explanations for why we would be conducting such interviews were much less readily accepted or grasped. In no case other than that of the Soviet Jews did people come forward to show their credentials in an attempt to join the research team.

Thus, interpreting the immigrants' approach to the interview situa-tion in cultural terms can be as meaningful as the actual content of the exchange. In the case of the former Soviet Jews, although they demon-strated an overall sympathy with the rationale of the project, other fac-tors made collecting their oral histories more challenging. The popula-tion is one that had lived their lives in terror of revealing their private feelings for fear of being reported to the government.

Similarly, comparative approaches to the question of timing and the logistics of the interview process itself can be indicative of economic cul-ture. With one exception, all the respondents from the Soviet Jewish community kept their appointments with me. The one individual who forgot called immediately to apologize. Theirs is a modern and rationalized sense of time and history. The experience of conducting research with the Haitian and Puerto Rican populations was quite different. Contacts were often late or did not show up at all. Rarely did respondents phone to confirm or cancel appointments. These are just a few examples of employing a comparative hermeneutic perspective to the research. It demands approaching the interview situation with respect for the respondents and the way they shape the process while potentially providing clues to the contexts from which these accounts of the self emerged.[12]

Notes

1. On the impact of the Second Great Awakening on the everyday life of the average businessman, Johnson (1978, 8) writes, "In 1825 a northern businessman dominated his wife and children, worked irregular hours, consumed enormous amounts of alcohol, and seldom voted or went to church. Ten years later the same man went to church twice a week, treated his family with gentleness and love, drank nothing but water, worked steady hours and forced his employees to do the same, campaigned for the Whig Party and spent his spare time convincing others that if they organized their lives in similar ways, the world would be perfect. To put it simply the middle class became resolutely bourgeois between 1825 and 1835. And at every step, that transformation bore the stamp of evangelical Protestantism."

2. See, for example, Mills 1951; Bottomore 1966.

3. Thanks to Ivan Light for this insight put forth in the discussion of papers presented at Ethnicity and the Entrepreneur: A Conference on New Immigrants in Business, Boston, 30 April–1 May 1992.

4. For an excellent example of how recent immigrants have reinvigorated a decaying neighborhood, see Louis Winnick's study (1990) of Brooklyn's Sunset Park.

5. The calculations for each of the four tables included in this chapter are based on weighted 5-percent PUMS data. In some instances, the samples are so small that their statistical validity may be questionable. This is particularly true of the poverty-level figure for the Greater Boston Metropolitan Area Cambodian population (table 4). Nonetheless, I have opted to include this number for rough comparative purposes.

6. The area population figures quoted in this discussion are from the 1990 U.S. census totals.

7. See, for example, Portes and Bach 1985, chap. 6; Cobas, Aickin, and Jardine 1992.

8. Ivan Light is currently investigating this question in his ongoing research into Korean entrepreneurship.

9. Silvia Pedraza is currently developing and refining a broad-based typology of the differing strategies utilized in an ethnic economy, which synthesizes much of the research in this field. She incorporates some of the types discussed here and is concerned with a wide variety of other ethnic groups as well.

10. For a lengthier discussion of the comparative advantages and disadvantages of refugee versus immigrant status, see Gold 1992, 17–22, 195–97.

11. See Bhachu 1985; Espiritu 1989.

12. For a thought-provoking discussion on the use of hermeneutics in analysis of subjective documents, see Yans-McLaughlin 1990; for an example of a similar approach to interviewing, although the author does not conceptualize his methodology in hermeneutic terms, see the Appendix in Redding 1990.

References

Bhachu, Parminder. 1985. *Twice Migrants: East African Sikh Settlers in Britain*. London: Tavistock.

Birch, David L. 1993. "Top States for Business Start-Ups." Cambridge, Mass.: Cognetics.

Bottomore, T. B. 1966. *Classes in Modern Society*. New York: Pantheon.

Butler, John Sibley. 1991. *Entrepreneurship and Self-Help among Black Americans: A Reconsideration of Race and Economics*. Albany: State University of New York Press.

Butler, John Sibley, and Cedric Herring. 1991. "Ethnicity and Entrepreneurship in America: Toward an Explanation of Racial and Ethnic Group Variations in Self-Employment." *Sociological Perspectives* 34, no. 1: 79–94.

Cobas, José, Mikel Aickin, and Douglas S. Jardine. 1992. "Industrial Segmentation, the Ethnic Economy, and Job Mobility: The Case of Cuban Exiles in Florida." Paper presented at the annual meeting of the American Sociological Association, Pittsburgh, 20–24 August.

Corey, Lewis H. 1966. "The Middle Class." In *Class, Status, and Power*, 2d ed. Edited by Reinhard Bendix and Seymour Lipset. Glencoe, Ill.: Free Press.

Espiritu, Yen Le. 1989. "Beyond the 'Boat People': Ethnicization of American Life." *Amerasia* 15, no. 2: 49–67.

Gold, Steve. 1992. *Refugee Communities: A Comparative Field Study*. Newbury Park, Calif.: Sage.

Johnson, Paul E. 1978. *A Shopkeeper's Millennium: Society and Revivals in Rochester, New York, 1815–1837*. New York: Hill and Wang.

Mandel, Michael, and Christopher Farrell. 1992. "The Immigrants: How They're Helping to Revitalize the U.S. Economy." *Business Week*, 13 July, 114.

Mills, C. W. 1951. *White Collar*. New York: Oxford University Press.

Model, Suzanne. 1993. "The Ethnic Niche and the Structure of Opportunity: Immigrants and Minorities in New York City." In *The "Underclass" Debate: Views from History*, edited by Michael B. Katz. Princeton: Princeton University Press.

Portes, Alejandro, and Robert Bach. 1985. *Latin Journey: Cuban and Mexican Immigrants in the United States*. Berkeley: University of California Press.

Redding, S. Gordon. 1990. *The Spirit of Chinese Capitalism*. Berlin and New York. Walter de Gruyter.

Ward, Robin, and Richard Jenkins. 1984. *Ethnic Communities in Business: Strategies for Economic Survival*. Cambridge: Cambridge University Press.

Winnick, Louis. 1990. *New People in Old Neighborhoods: The Role of New Immi-*

grants in Rejuvenating New York's Communities. New York: Russell Sage Foundation.

Yans-McLaughlin, Virginia. 1990. "Metaphors of Self in History: Subjectivity, Oral Narrative, and Immigration Studies." In *Immigration Reconsidered: History, Sociology, and Politics,* edited by Yans-McLaughlin. New York: Oxford University Press.

Chapter 2

Ethnic Economy or Ethnic Enclave Economy?

Ivan Light, Georges Sabagh,

Mehdi Bozorgmehr,

and Claudia Der-Martirosian

Dual labor market theory developed in the late 1960s as an effort to explain persistent inequality in employment (Averitt 1968). Seeking to explain the reduced income and status attainment of women and minorities, dual labor market theory claimed that disadvantaged groups were locked into an inferior, secondary labor market that did not permit egress into the more desirable, primary labor market (Beck, Horan, and Tolbert 1978; Tolbert, Horan, and Beck 1980). "Labor market segmentation" meant the long-term coexistence of noncommunicating labor markets in which vastly different standards of remuneration and work satisfaction prevailed. Because neoclassical economics declared such a situation impossible, labor segmentation theorists had to concentrate on proof, not theory. Valid as far as it went, dual labor market theory took wage labor as its employment universe, overlooking minority self-employment on the grounds, then widely believed, that self-employment was a dwindling phenomenon of negligible importance. In practice, this simplification led to a worldview in which self-employment vanished from the consciousness of social scientists.

Sullivan (1981, 342) was among the first to note that labor market studies could no longer treat self-employment as an "anomaly" that could safely be ignored. Somewhat later, Portes and Manning (1986) made the case more forcefully, and their view has subsequently prevailed. Although some segmentation theorists still ignore self-employment without explanation (Sakamoto and Chen 1991), or in Mar's case (1991, 13) in the interest of theoretical consistency, informed opinion no longer mistakes such a treatment for a comprehensive analysis of employment. First, self-employment is not declining anymore in North America or in Western Europe (Light and Sanchez 1987, 376; Ward 1987, 161). Second, its prevalence was long underestimated in official documents, a practice that, it is now recognized, unwisely encouraged social scientists to ignore the phenomenon (Borjas 1986, 486; Light and Bonacich 1988, 10–11). Finally, the effects of self-employment are much stronger in immigrant and ethnic minority communities than they are in the general economy (Light 1984). Therefore, even if inconsequential outside the minority communities, self-employment remains consequential within them.

As currently understood, the primary and secondary sectors of the general labor market coexist with an immigrant-owned business sector in which immigrants work as employees of coethnics or as entrepreneurs (Bailey and Waldinger 1991). The size of the immigrant sector is variable, as is its formality. That is, some immigrant groups have large business sectors, some small. In some groups, the immigrant business sector is primarily formal, in others primarily informal (Light, Bhachu, and Karageorgis 1992). Either way, immigrants find employment in the general labor market or in the immigrant business sector; they switch back and forth between the sectors; and they trade off the costs and benefits of employment in either sector.

Lieberson and Waters (1988, 135–36) declare it "difficult to overstate the importance of income" in studies of racial and ethnic relations. In complete agreement with this observation, most current sociology approaches those trade-offs in terms of employee returns on human capital. It is generally conceded that the self-employed earn higher returns on their human capital than do their peers who work for wages and salaries in the general labor market.[1] However, a controversy rages about the relative advantageousness of the ethnic enclave economy for coethnics employed in it. Some writers have argued that employees earn higher human capital-adjusted returns in the ethnic enclave economy than do their counterparts in the secondary or even the primary labor market (Portes and Bach 1985, 226–39). Others have argued that only the entrepreneurs earn higher returns in the ethnic enclave economy; their employees earn lower returns than they would in the general labor market (Nee and Sanders 1987; Johnson 1988, 17). Zhou and Logan (1989) claim that sometimes one, sometimes the other pattern prevails depending on locality, gender, and specific group affiliations. Model (1992,

78) finds no difference between the returns to labor in the ethnic enclave economy and the general labor market.

We do not propose to debate this question and, in fact, regard its salience as the misguided product of terminological confusion occasioned by the abrupt and disconcerting rediscovery of self-employment, the collapse of labor segmentation theory, and the rush to fill the theoretical void that ensued (Light and Bonacich 1988, ix–xiv). This theoretical confusion arises, we agree, from uncritical adoption of the concept of the ethnic enclave economy (Cobas 1986, 1989; Kim and Hurh 1990). We maintain that this concept is of more limited value in social research than its current centrality warrants. Moreover, if the theoretical issue is carefully addressed in the light of easily accessible evidence, the terms of the whole debate change.

The Ethnic Economy

To establish this claim, we have to review the history of the concept of ethnic enclave economy, first contrasting it with the ethnic economy, its conceptual pair. The concept of ethnic economy derived from the historical sociology of Max Weber and Werner Sombart (Light and Karageorgis 1994, 647) and, following them, from the literature of middleman minorities (Zenner 1991). Model (1992, 64) claims that Bonacich (1973) was "the first to examine the definitive characteristics" of the ethnic economy. Her claim is wrong in two senses. First, Bonacich (1973) addressed middleman minorities, not the ethnic economy, and the literature of middleman minorities considerably antedates her 1973 discussion. Second, Bonacich (1973) did not define the concept of ethnic economy, nor even use the words in her text. The concept of ethnic economy split away from the parent concept of middleman minority seven years after Bonacich's influential article appeared. True, Modell (1977, 94) used the term "ethnic economy" to describe "a kind of ethnic-based welfare capitalism" among Japanese Americans before World War II. This is the first use of the term that we know, and this use clearly fed into the later formulation. But Modell (1977) did not operationally define the concept of ethnic economy.

Bonacich and Modell (1980, 45) were the first operationally to define the concept of ethnic economy. By ethnic economy, they meant the self-employed and their coethnic employees (Bonacich and Modell 1980, 110–11, 124). They identified the ethnic economy of a city, region, or nation, but an ethnic economy always included all workers in these two categories and excluded workers whose employers were not coethnics. In this sense, the Cuban ethnic economy of Miami would comprise self-employed Cubans and their Cuban employees in Miami. It would not include Cubans who worked for wages in the general economy, or non-Cuban employees of Cuban-owned firms.

Thus defined, an ethnic economy is ethnic simply because the personnel (owners and employees) are coethnics. Bonacich and Modell's concept of ethnic economy made no claims about the locational clustering or density of firms that might, indeed, be evenly distributed among neighborhoods and industries. As a matter of definition, their concept also made no claims about the level of ethnicity within the ethnic economy or between buyers and sellers. This definition did not, for example, require or direct attention to trade conducted by owners for the benefit of coethnic buyers, whether at the retail or wholesale level (Bonacich and Modell 1980, 111). Owners were in their own group's ethnic economy regardless of whether their customers were coethnics. Nor did their concept of ethnic economy require or assume an ethnic cultural ambience within the firm or among sellers and buyers. That ambience was an empirical product of Bonacich and Modell's research (1980); they found that those in the Japanese American ethnic economy were more ethnically Japanese than Japanese Americans of the same generation who worked in the general labor market. This empirical result was not, however, a matter of definition. The Japanese ethnic economy would have remained an ethnic economy even had the workers demonstrated no higher ethnicity than Japanese Americans outside it.

Describing "segregated work settings," Reitz (1980, 154–56) used a related but slightly different definition in his research on immigrants in Toronto. Like Bonacich and Modell, Reitz included the self-employed and their coethnic employees in his concept; but unlike Bonacich and Modell, he also added all workplaces in which coethnic employees spoke their native language on the job rather than English. If employees of the telephone company spoke a foreign language on the job, then Reitz added them to the immigrant work setting. Therefore, Reitz's formula was *self-employed + coethnic employees + all other employees who speak their native tongue, a foreign language, on the job.*

By adding the third term, Reitz's definition increased the size of the ethnic economy because workers may speak their native language on the job but not be employed by a coethnic. However, Reitz's addition muddied the conceptual clarity of the ethnic economy. Because speaking a foreign language at work is itself a standard measure of ethnicity, some inhabitants of Reitz's ethnic economy were likely to be more ethnic than coethnics by dint of the definition of ethnic work setting. Therefore, an ethnic economy would have to be more ethnic than the general economy. However, like Bonacich and Modell, Reitz kept his concept free of locational clustering and coethnic customers. Additionally, he *treated* his definition of ethnic economy as if it were free of contamination by ethnic behavior built into the concept. Reitz's concept of ethnic work setting is arguably superior to that of Bonacich and Modell. The issue has never been addressed, and we do not propose to do so here, on the grounds that Reitz's concept has been less influential in framing the terms of the current debate.

The Ethnic Enclave Economy

The literature of the ethnic enclave economy has a different derivation from that of the ethnic economy. Unlike the literature of the ethnic economy, which derived from the earlier literature of middleman minorities, the ethnic enclave economy derived from dual labor market theory, itself a product of institutional economics (Averitt 1968). This origin is clear in Wilson and Portes (1980), the earliest formulation of the ethnic enclave economy. After a review of the dual labor markets literature, to which they believed themselves to be contributors, Wilson and Portes (1980, 297–302) introduced the concept of "immigrant enclave," a conceptual ancestor of the ethnic enclave economy. By immigrant enclave, however, they still meant only the employment of immigrant workers in "the enclave labor market." Workers were in the enclave labor market if their employers were coethnics (Wilson and Portes 1980, 306–7). Wilson and Portes did not include the self-employed in their study because only workers were of interest to students of labor market segmentation—and the self-employed were not workers because they did not earn wages.

In a subsequent seminal publication, Portes (1981) expanded the enclave labor market to include the self-employed, the first time dual labor market theorists had done so. According to Portes, immigrant enclaves had two characteristics: spatial clustering and numerous immigrant-owned business firms that employed numerous coethnic workers.[2] "Enclaves consist of immigrant groups which concentrate in a distinct spatial location and organize a variety of enterprises serving their own ethnic market and/or the general population. Their basic characteristic is that a significant proportion of the immigrant labor force works in enterprises owned by other immigrants" (Portes 1981, 290–91).

As this text makes clear, even though his new conceptualization included the self-employed, then a conceptual innovation, Portes's emphasis was still on the numerous workers they employed, not on the self-employed themselves.[3] This emphasis on numerous workers was a product of the labor market segmentation tradition from which Portes derived. It clearly sidestepped the question of what was to be done with the self-employed who employed no workers.

Portes and Bach (1985, 203) returned to Portes's earlier definition (1981) of an enclave economy. However, they operationalized the Cuban enclave economy as "all men indicating employment in firms owned by Cubans," a definition that excluded the self-employed (Portes and Bach 1985, 217). Later, aggregating self-employed and their coethnic employees, who were not further distinguished, their final operationalization actually followed Bonacich and Modell's earlier definition (1980) of the ethnic economy even though it contradicted the definition of enclave economy they offered. In this book, the ethnic enclave economy empirically consisted of the self-employed plus their coethnic employees in Miami. They compared Cuban workers in the enclave economy with Cuban workers in the primary and secondary sectors of the labor market in respect to money returns on human capital. They found that after six years of residence in the United States, the Cuban immigrants' money returns on occupational prestige and knowledge of English were more favorable in the enclave than in the primary labor market (Portes and Bach 1985, 235–36).

Turning to Mexican immigrant men, whom they also followed longitudinally from their arrival, Portes and Bach (1985, 267–68) found no enclave economy at all, a telling result. Cubans had an ethnic enclave economy, and Mexicans did not. Of course, Portes and Bach found self-employment among Mexican immigrants in their sample. In 1979, 5.5 percent of Mexican immigrant men in their sample were self-employed, compared to 21.2 percent of Cuban men (Portes and Bach 1985, 187, 193). However, for some reason, they decided that Mexican self-employment did not create a small immigrant enclave economy to contrast with the Cubans' big one. Such a position would have coincided with the treatment one would have expected from the perspective of Bonacich and Modell's concept of ethnic economy. Instead, they declared that Cubans had an enclave economy and Mexicans did not have one. As a result, Mexican immigrants had to take their chances as "low wage labor in the open economy," whereas Cubans operated in a "setting dominated by immigrant business networks" (Portes and Bach 1985, 338, 268). The nonexistence of a Mexican enclave economy is clear evidence that Portes and Bach's concepts were not the same as those earlier introduced by Bonacich and Modell.

Although Portes and Bach (1985, 370) cited Bonacich and Modell (1980), thus indicating familiarity with this earlier work, in their treatment of Mexicans they presumably diverged from this concept of ethnic economy because they wanted to propose something different. As Portes and Bach (1985, 217) conceived it, the ethnic enclave economy was not just the coethnic self-employed and their coethnic employees. It also consisted of a *locational cluster* of business firms whose owners and employees were coethnics and whose firms employed a "significant number" of coethnic workers. From this definition, three corollaries followed that presumably excluded the Mexicans from an ethnic enclave economy, even though they clearly had an ethnic economy as Bonacich and Modell (1980) would have defined it. First, unlike Cubans in their sample, 90 percent of whom resided in Miami, Mexicans in their sample were more evenly dispersed across the Southwest. Therefore, their ethnic economies were small in scale and could not derive the same benefits from locational aggregation. Second, the scattered Mexican ethnic economies lacked a huge locational cluster like Miami's Little Havana. Third, the Mexican self-employed presumably did not employ a significant number of coethnics in their firms, most of which had no employees at all. For these reasons, Mexicans had an ethnic economy as Bonacich and Modell (1980) had defined it, but they did not have an ethnic enclave economy as Portes and Bach defined it (Hansen and Cardenas 1988).

When defining the ethnic enclave economy, Portes and Bach had in mind the Cuban economy of Miami. One-half the population of Miami is of Cuban origin. Miami's Little Havana contained (and still contains) a conspicuous concentration of Cuban-owned firms in which many Cuban employees worked (and still work). The concentration of the firms in a Cuban business district was conceptually important because of the threshold benefits supposedly derived therefrom. That is, Wilson and Portes (1980, 301–2) and Wilson and Martin (1982, 138) had argued that the Cuban ethnic enclave economy was hyperefficient because of vertical and horizontal integration, ethnically sympathetic suppliers and consumers, pooled savings, and rigged markets. Not sharing in this agglomeration benefit, Cuban-owned firms outside the Cuban enclave presumably did not derive any spin-off benefit from their location, so the enclave concept appropriately excluded such firms and their Cuban employees. Indeed, the alleged agglomeration effects of the Cuban ethnic enclave in Miami explained why immigrant Mexicans could not obtain rates of self-employment as high as did immigrant Cubans (Portes and Bach 1985, 267–68).

Although we agree with the overall conclusion of Portes and Bach, who offered a persuasive explanation of why working-class Cuban men earned more six years after arrival in the United States than did working-class Mexican men, we think that, when they ignored the Mexican self-employed, they made a conceptual error. As a partial result of their conceptualization of the ethnic enclave economy, torturously unraveled above, "there is no agreement about what an ethnic enclave is" (Gilbertson, Waldinger, and Gurak 1990). Kim and Hurh (1990) even complain that Portes and Jensen (1989) abandoned the original concept of ethnic enclave economy, thus rendering the concept "useless." This conceptual anarchy has encouraged researchers to define the ethnic enclave economy to suit themselves, thus further increasing the terminological confusion (Model 1985, 1992; Fernandez-Kelly and Garcia 1989, 248; Boyd 1989; Mar 1991). For example, Gold (1992, 109) declares that the "most central feature" of an ethnic enclave is "the ability of its entrepreneurs to sell goods and services" to outsiders. The concept of ethnic enclave economy has become a rubber yardstick.

Relative Earnings

Partially as a result of the fuzziness in the original concept of ethnic enclave economy, subsequent debates have lopsidedly fastened on the issue of relative wages (Sanders and Nee 1987; Jiobu 1988; Portes and Jensen 1989; Zhou and Logan 1989; Gilbertson, Waldinger, and Gurak 1990; Model 1992, 63). Relative wages means employee returns on human capital inside and outside the ethnic enclave economy. Portes and Bach (1985) found that human capital-adjusted wages in the ethnic enclave economy equalled or exceeded those in the primary labor market. Model (1992, 65) labels this claim the "enclave economy hypothesis."

Rejecting the enclave economy hypothesis, Sanders and Nee (1987, 747–48, 758) argued that these results arose from aggregating the money income of enclave employers and their employees. This issue led to a concentration on whether residence or work address should be used in defining participation in the ethnic enclave economy (Portes and Jensen 1987). Other authors have subsequently entered this debate with inconsistent results that do not permit any overall conclusion about relative wages (Jiobu 1988; Zhou and Logan 1989; Model 1992).[4] Admittedly, this issue merits some attention. However, lopsided attention to it has obscured, in our mind, the more fundamental issue of what is an ethnic enclave economy and how does it differ from an ethnic economy?

The lopsided focus of the current debate on relative wages derives from the enclave literature's origin in labor segmentation theory as well as its protracted and continuing uncertainty about whether or how to treat self-employment. With the exception of Zhou and Logan (1989), all the participants in this debate have concentrated wholly on relative wages, altogether neglecting the self-employed. On the positive side, the labor segmentation literature introduced the custom of making earnings comparisons that were adjusted for differences in human capital. On the negative side, however, the labor segmentation tradition bequeathed a willingness to ignore self-employment in order to concentrate on labor issues. The importance of the debate about relative earnings rests upon the assumption that employees are more numerous than the self-employed. If this assumption held, then the economic contribution of the ethnic economy to a group's aggregate income would depend more upon the earnings of enclave employees than upon those of the enclave self-employed. The general labor market contains ten employees for every one self-employed, so the earnings of the employed largely determine the earnings of the whole group. However, numbers in the ethnic economy are reversed. In the ethnic economy, the self-employed outnumber the employees by three to two. This imbalance arises because employer firms are only about one-fifth of all minority firms, and because employer firms are small.

Table 1 shows the number of minority-owned business firms in the United States in 1987, distinguishing firms owned by blacks, Hispanics, and Asians and Pacific Islanders. Among the employer firms, average employment was 3.4 workers per firm. Therefore, the employees were more numerous than the employers by a ratio of about three to one.[5] But 80 percent of minority-owned firms had no employees. Comparing the

Table 1. Minority-Owned Firms in the United States, 1987

	Total Number of Firms	Firms with Employees		
		Number of Firms	% of All Firms	Number of Employees
Black	424,165	70,815	16.7	220,464
Hispanic	422,373	89,908	21.3	264,846
Asian & Pacific Islander	355,331	92,718	26.1	351,345
Other Minority[a]	1,213,750	248,149	20.4	836,483

Source: U.S. Department of Commerce, Bureau of the Census, *1987 Economic Censuses. MB87-4. Survey of Minority-Owned Business Enterprise. Summary* (Washington D.C.: U.S. Government Printing Office, 1991), table 1.
[a] Includes groups not shown separately.

number of all minority-owned firms with the number of their employees, we find that employees were only 69 percent as numerous as the firms (see table 1).

Number of firms offers a very conservative estimate of the number of coethnic self-employed. After all, some of these minority-owned firms had multiple owners, and in many firms, unpaid family members had an ownership stake as well. Therefore, to estimate the number of owners based on the number of firms (1 firm = 1 owner) is to underestimate the true number of owners. On the other side, the total number of employees overestimates the number of coethnic employees. Some employees of minority-owned firms are not coethnics. Therefore, they do not participate in the ethnic economy as defined above.

Although these statistics are only approximate, they demonstrate the distortion caused by concentrating on the earnings of employees and neglecting the self-employed. Obviously the income effect of the ethnic economy depends on the aggregated earnings of self-employed, employers, and employees, not just or even mainly the last. Conceding that the self-employed obtain better human capital-adjusted returns than do coethnics employed for wages and salaries in the general labor market, Sanders and Nee (1987, 746–48) claimed that low relative wages in the ethnic economy invalidate a favorable judgment about the economic benefit of an enclave economy.[6] Because Portes and his associates had advanced exactly this claim, the debate about relative earnings was mistaken for a test of this issue. Disputants assumed that if the enclave economy's wages were relatively lower than those paid in the general labor market, then the enclave was an obstacle to the economic advancement of any group, not a benefit (Model 1992, 63).

In reality, a final judgment hinges on the relative numbers of the self-employed, employers, and coethnic employees. The smaller the share of coethnic employees in the total personnel of the ethnic economy, the less significant their relative earnings. In an extreme case, when an ethnic economy contains no employees at all, the issue of relative wages becomes meaningless. In general, since the self-employed are much more numerous than their employees, the economic benefit of the ethnic economy depends more on the earnings of the self-employed than on the wages of their coethnic employees. If the relative wages of the self-employed exceed those of employees in the general labor market, and the self-employed are more numerous than the enclave employees, then the overall economic effect of the enclave might be positive even if relative wages in the enclave were less than those in the general labor market.

Bringing Unemployment Back In

Worse, even if we assume that relative wages in the general labor market are much higher than those in the ethnic enclave, although evidence on this point is inconclusive, it does not follow that wage employment in the ethnic economy is disadvantageous. Those ethnic economy employees who can obtain higher paying jobs in the general labor market may do so. No one constrains their freedom of choice. Therefore, their presence at low wages is mute evidence that they do not know of more desirable earning opportunities in the general labor market or that, knowing about them, they chose the ethnic economy despite its low wages.[7] The ethnic economy is, after all, culturally sympathetic. Of the Chinese garment factories in New York City, Wong (1987, 129) wrote that "ethnic values impel the employers to adhere to certain cultural rules and etiquette." He wrote also that "ideas of a common destiny, common ethnic origin, and same people help to reduce conflicts and promote workers' identification with the firm" (Wong 1987, 128). To the extent that these nonmonetary issues matter to workers, they might prefer to work in a culturally sympathetic firm even if they know about higher paying jobs in the mainstream economy.

33

Research has repetitively found that many wage workers in the ethnic economy become self-employed later (Light 1972, 67; Portes and Bach 1985; Cobas, Aickin, and Jardine 1992). In effect, the ethnic economy is a school for entrepreneurs. When they open businesses of their own, former employees of coethnics increase their own and their community's income and wealth. Comparing wages outside and inside the ethnic economy, critics who overlook this educational function overlook the long-term benefit. One might equally well object to high school attendance on the grounds that employed dropouts earn more than students, who earn nothing. However, once graduated, the students will earn more than the dropouts. Therefore, an economic objection to high school attendance must not overlook its long-range economic benefit, focusing only on the opportunity cost of completing the program. Insofar as the ethnic economy trains entrepreneurs, a focus on relative wages falls into exactly this fallacy.

Jobs have working conditions as well as paychecks, and often working conditions are critical to employment (Model 1992, 80). Many employees in ethnic economies are women who cannot or do not wish to work full time because of their child care responsibilities.[8] Like other employers in the informal sector, coethnic employers often permit women employees to watch their children while at work, thus freeing women to work who would otherwise be unemployed. That is, if a woman must mind her children while she works, and she cannot find a job in the general labor market that permits her to accomplish this task, then the general labor market offers this woman no employment. That woman's ability to earn any wage then depends on an ethnic economy within which employers relax the "no children" formalism of the general labor market (Perez 1986). In such a case, even if a woman earns much lower human capital-adjusted wages than do her peers in the general labor market, as Zhou and Logan (1989, 817–18) report, she earns more than zero. Since zero earnings is what the general labor market offers the unemployed, a low-wage job in the ethnic economy benefits this woman.

The same resolute ignoring of underemployment and unemployment characterizes Sanders and Nee's comparison (1987) of the aggregate income effects of the ethnic enclave economy. To compare relative wages is to assume that the general labor market offers only jobs to job-seekers so that the alternative to a job in the ethnic economy is a job in the general labor market. In reality, the general labor market offers job-seekers jobs, underemployment, and unemployment. That is, a person who sets out to find a job in the general labor market may wind up unemployed or working less than full time when full-time employment is desired. Therefore, whenever unemployment and underemployment exist in the general economy, and directly proportional to their extent, an ethnic economy increases the aggregate income of a minority group *even if* everyone in it (self-employed, employers, employees) earns a lower human capital-adjusted return than do coethnics in the general labor market. Moreover, as Bridges and Villemez (1991, 758) have shown, realistic self-employment options increase the income of wage earners whose employers must pay them more in order to forestall their loss to self-employment. Therefore, a large ethnic economy tends to raise the wages of coethnics employed in the general labor market.

The African American Ethnic Economy

To illustrate this point with evidence, and to facilitate comprehension of the argument, table 2 juxtaposes the employment profile of blacks and whites in 1987. Blacks are not essential to this argument. Any minority could have been compared with whites and the results would have been

Table 2. Workers in the U.S. Nonagricultural Labor Force, 1987

	Whites		Blacks	
	Number (in 1,000s)	%	Number (in 1,000s)	%
General Labor Market				
Wage and Salary	86,983	86.7	10,769	83.9
Unemployed	5,501	5.5	1,684	13.1
Ethnic Economy				
Self-Employed	7,586	7.6	369	2.9
Unpaid Family Workers	233	0.2	7	0.1
Total	100,303	100	12,829	100

Source: U.S. Department of Commerce, Bureau of Labor Statistics. *Labor Force Statistics Derived from the Current Population Survey, 1948–87*. Bulletin 2307 (Washington D.C.: U.S. Government Printing Office, 1988), tables A24 and B11.
Note: Numbers are for workers sixteen years of age or older.

Table 3. Blacks in the U.S. Nonagricultural Labor Force, 1987

	Observed		Hypothetical	
	Number (in 1,000s)	%	Number (in 1,000s)	%
General Labor Market				
Wage and Salary	10,769	83.9	10,837[a]	84.5
Unemployed	1,684	13.1	1,485[b]	11.6
Ethnic Economy				
Self-Employed	369	2.9	500	3.9
Unpaid Family Workers	7	0.1	7	0.1
Total	12,829	100.0	12,829	100.0

Source: U.S. Department of Commerce, Bureau of Labor Statistics, *Labor Force Statistics Derived from the Current Population Survey, 1948-87*. Bulletin 2307 (Washington, D.C.: U.S. Government Printing Office, 1988), tables A24 and B11.
[a] The additional black self-employed would generate some employees. The average employees for black self-employed in 1987 was 220,464 / 424,165 = 0.52 (see table 1). The additional 131,000 black self-employed would generate 68,120 additional wage and salary workers.
[b] Unemployment is reduced by the 131,000 unemployed who became self-employed and by the 68,120 unemployed who became employed by these 131,000 self-employed.

similar. The earnings disadvantage of blacks resides first and foremost in the unfavorable distribution of black workers among the four employment categories. Compared to whites, blacks had more unemployed who earned nothing. Compared to whites, blacks had fewer self-employed and employees who earned something. Even though blacks were paid less than whites for comparable work in 1987, a lugubrious fact, aggregate black income would have increased if black workers could have been shifted from unemployment into self-employment and wage employment. This improvement occurs because it is better to earn something than nothing.[9]

Following this observation, table 3 shows the expected changes in black employment that would arise from a hypothetical increase in black self-employment. The hypothetical result shows that, although black unemployment remains higher than that for whites, there is a reduction of about 18 percent in black unemployment. No matter how inferior the relative human capital-adjusted earnings of salaried blacks in the ethnic economy, even if self-employed blacks and their black employees both earned only one-tenth as much in the ethnic economy as their coethnic peers in the general labor market, the aggregate income of the black population would be increased by this hypothetical increase in black self-employment, the sympathetic increase in employment that increase would occasion, and the reduction of black unemployment (see table 3).

Admittedly, this conclusion depends on the claim that a 1 percent increase in self-employment and a sympathetic increase in coethnic wage employment in the black ethnic economy would come *wholly* from the ranks of unemployed blacks, reducing those ranks. If the new black entrepreneurs and their black employees were recruited from the black wage earners of the general economy, then this conclusion would not follow. But this objection only highlights the strength of this argument. Precisely because the earnings of black self-employed, employers, and their coethnic employees are inferior to those earned by blacks in the general labor market, we must assume that *only unemployed blacks* would be available to work in the black ethnic economy.[10] Otherwise, black workers would be moving from better paid wage and salary jobs in the general economy to poorly remunerated jobs in the ethnic economy. Therefore, even under the most disadvantageous earnings assumptions, the ethnic economy makes a positive contribution to the economic welfare of groups that are suffering underemployment and unemployment.[11] Relative earnings in the ethnic economy only affect how beneficial the ethnic economy is; they do not affect *whether* it is beneficial. The frantic empirical debate about relative wages is unnecessary to establish this conclusion, and no empirical data would reverse it short of the elimination of unemployment and underemployment.[12]

Although frequently confused or used interchangeably, the ethnic enclave economy and the ethnic economy are conceptually different. The concepts originated in different literatures, and they import different problematics into the research agenda. The fascination of the ethnic enclave literature with the unproductive issue of relative wages exemplifies this difference. The fascination is misguided because the self-employed are more numerous than their coethnic employees and because no matter how low the money returns actually are in the ethnic economy, they exceed what the unemployed earn in the general labor market.

The overlap of ethnic economy and ethnic enclave economy is imperfect. The ethnic economy is a much broader and more generally useful concept than is the ethnic enclave economy. Every immigrant group or ethnic minority has an ethnic economy, but only a few have an ethnic enclave economy. Because ethnic firms are small, the coethnic self-employed are more numerous than their coethnic employees. Hence, to stress the human capital-adjusted returns of employees in the ethnic enclave economy diverts attention from the main income effect to a subsidiary income effect.

Unless the conceptual issues are clearly specified, researchers will overlook and exclude most of the phenomena of interest because concepts do not fit what they see. Specifically, when ethnic firms are not clustered conspicuously in a neighborhood like Little Havana and when firm owners are more numerous than coethnic employees, then an ethnic economy will exist that does not fit the prevailing researcher conception of an ethnic enclave economy and so cannot be dealt with using this concept.[13]

We know of no case in which an ethnic enclave economy existed but an ethnic economy did not, and such a case would be conceptually impossible anyway. Without questioning the utility of the concept of ethnic enclave economy in these cases, such as the Cuban enclave in Miami, we nonetheless conclude that it is a special case of the ethnic economy, and that the ethnic economy is the more universal of the two concepts. Arguably, the progress of research depends on elaborating even more special cases to illuminate issues that the universal concept of ethnic economy leaves in darkness.

In our opinion, the ethnic economy is a universal conceptual tool suitable for most studies of immigrant and ethnic minority business enterprise. This concept avoids the misspecified debates about where respondents reside or work, thus facilitating data collection and research. It also extends the range of research to a much broader class of phenomena and is, indeed, universal and exportable. We concede the ethnic enclave economy's utility for specialized research that needs to take account of the distinction between enclave and nonenclave, but we believe that this research will be more successful if it understands its orienting concept as a special case of the ethnic economy.

Notes

1. This is not the same as claiming that the self-employed earn more than do wage and salary workers. On average, they do not. Among whites, blacks, and Hispanics, the self-employed earned less in 1987 than did wage and salary workers. See U.S. Department of Commerce, Bureau of the Census, *Survey of Minority Owned Business Enterprise. Summary* (Washington, D.C.: U.S. Government Printing Office, 1991), table 1, 14; ibid., *Money Incomes of Households, Families, and Persons in the U.S., 1990.* Series P-60 (Washington, D.C.: U.S. Government Printing Office, 1992), table 34.

2. This theme reappears in Portes and Manning (1986, 63): "The enclave is concentrated and spatially identifiable."

3. Wilson and Martin (1982) redefined Portes's concept of enclave economy. In order to permit intergroup comparisons, they developed an input-output model that permitted estimation of the extent to which vertical integration of firms permitted an enclave economy to capture re-spending. Although no one has subsequently followed up this line of research, their emphasis on compact interdependence did become a permanent feature of the enclave literature.

4. Portes and Jensen (1987) claimed that Sanders and Nee's selection (1987) of external residence as a measure of participation in the general labor market permitted them to compare suburban and inner city wage earners, thus creating the misleading impression that the relative earnings in the ethnic enclave were lower. In the conceptual free-for-all, Mar (1991, 7) even reinvented the concept of ethnic economy, calling it an "ethnic labor market" in apparent ignorance of Bonacich and Modell's prior terminology (1980).

5. These are the best data available, but they underestimate the contribution of the largest firms to employment. Based on a survey of proprietorships, partnerships, and corporations with ten or fewer shareholders, the data in table 1 pertain only to small and medium-size firms.

6. Income understates the economic advantage of the self-employed. Oliver and Shapiro (1990, 143–44) have shown that the self-employed own "from two to 14 times as much net worth as their salaried counterparts." This superiority is much greater than any superiority in income.

7. "As members of an ethnic group, however, the information seeking of Koreans . . . is largely confined within their ethnic information environment" (Yoon, 1992, 202).

8. In Los Angeles, immigrant Mexican and Central American women provided the principal labor force for Asian-owned garment manufacturing firms (Zentgraf 1989, 127). Although these Asian-owned garment factories participated in the informal economy, they did not belong in the Mexican or Central American ethnic economies as Bonacich and Modell earlier defined that concept.

9. In actuality, unemployed blacks do not earn nothing because so many participate in the informal economy in which they are *self-employed*. Loic Wacquant (in press, 9) lists and enumerates the kinds of businesses that unemployed and underemployed blacks operated in Chicago.

10. If black employers hire nonblack employees, they add no employment to the black ethnic economy. Whether they pay these nonblack employees well or badly then makes no difference to the economic welfare of blacks.

11. If workers in the ethnic economy earn more than do coethnics in the general

labor market, then every time workers move from the general labor market to the ethnic economy, the aggregate income of their group increases. When workers make this advantageous move, they leave behind a vacancy in the general labor market that may be filled by an unemployed coethnic.

12. If we had assumed that the workers in the ethnic economy earned higher relative returns than their counterparts in the general economy, there would have been no necessity for conducting this whole exercise as the ethnic economy would obviously have raised the earnings of the whole group: the bigger the ethnic economy, the richer the group.

13. See Joel Garreau, "Area Koreans See No Need for Enclaves," *Washington Post*, 11 January 1992.

References

Averitt, Robert T. 1968. *The Dual Economy*. New York: Norton.

Bailey, Thomas, and Roger Waldinger. 1991. "Primary, Secondary, and Enclave Labor Markets: A Training Systems Approach." *American Sociological Review* 56: 432–45.

Beck, E. M., Patrick M. Horan, and Charles M. Tolbert. 1978. "Stratification in the Dual Economy: A Sectoral Model of Earnings Determination." *American Sociological Review* 43: 704–20.

Bonacich, Edna. 1973. "A Theory of Middleman Minorities." *American Sociological Review* 38: 583–94.

Bonacich, Edna, and John Modell. 1980. *The Economic Basis of Ethnic Solidarity*. Berkeley: University of California Press.

Borjas, George J. 1986. "The Self-Employment Experience of Immigrants." *Journal of Human Resources* 21: 486–506.

Boyd, Monica. 1989. "Family and Personal Networks in International Migration." *International Migration Review* 23: 638–69.

Bridges, William P., and Wayne J. Villemez. 1991. "Employment Relations and the Labor Market: Integrating Institutional and Market Perspectives." *American Sociological Review* 56: 748–64.

Cobas, Jose. 1986. "Paths to Self-Employment among Immigrants." *Sociological Perspectives* 29: 101–20.

——. 1989. "Six Problems in the Sociology of the Ethnic Economy." *Sociological Perspectives* 32: 201–14.

Cobas, Jose A., Mikel Aickin, and Douglas S. Jardine. 1992. "Industrial Segmentation, The Ethnic Economy, and Job Mobility: The Case of Cuban Exiles in Florida." Paper presented at the annual meeting of the American Sociological Association, Pittsburgh, 20–24 August.

Fernandez-Kelly, M. Patricia, and Anna M. Garcia. 1989. "Informalization at the Core: Hispanic Women, Homework, and the Advanced Capitalist State." Chap. 13 in *The Informal Economy*, edited by Alejandro Portes, Manuel Castells, and Lauren A. Benton. Baltimore: Johns Hopkins University Press.

Gilbertson, Greta, Roger Waldinger, and Douglas T. Gurak. 1990. "When It's Bad to Have a Coethnic Boss." Paper presented at the annual meeting of the American Sociological Association, Washington, D.C., 11–15 August.

Gold, Steven. 1992. *Refugee Communities: A Comparative Field Study*. Newbury Park, Calif.: Sage.

Hansen, Niles H., and Gilberto Cardenas. 1988. "Immigrant and Native Ethnic Enterprises in Mexican American Neighborhoods." *International Migration Review* 22: 226–42.

Jiobu, Robert. 1988. "Ethnic Hegemony and the Japanese of California." *American Sociological Review* 53: 353–67.

Johnson, Phyllis J. 1988. "The Impact of Ethnic Communities on the Employment of Southeast Asian Refugees." *Amerasia* 14: 1–22.

Kim, Kwang Chung, and Won Moo Hurh. 1990. "Immigrants' Ethnic Enclave: Its Conceptual Issues." Paper presented at the annual meeting of American Sociological Association, Washington, D.C., 11–15 August.

Lieberson, Stanley, and Mary C. Waters. 1988. *From Many Strands: Ethnic and Racial Groups in Contemporary America.* New York: Russell Sage.

Light, Ivan. 1972. *Ethnic Enterprise in America.* Berkeley: University of California Press.

———. 1984. "Immigrant and Ethnic Enterprise in North America." *Ethnic and Racial Studies* 7: 195–216.

Light, Ivan, Parminder Bhachu, and Stavros Karageorgis. 1992. "Entrepreneurship and Immigrant Networks." Chap. 2 in *Immigration and Entrepreneurship,* edited by Ivan Light and Parminder Bhachu. New Brunswick, N.J.: Transaction.

Light, Ivan, and Edna Bonacich. 1988. *Immigrant Entrepreneurs: Koreans in Los Angeles, 1965–1982.* Berkeley: University of California Press.

Light, Ivan, and Stavros Karageorgis. 1994. "The Ethnic Economy." Chap. 26 in *The Handbook of Economic Sociology,* edited by Neil Smelser and Richard Swedberg. Princeton: Princeton University Press.

Light, Ivan, and Angel Sanchez. 1987. "Immigrant Entrepreneurs in 272 SMSAs." *Sociological Perspectives* 30: 373–99.

Mar, Don. 1991. "Another Look at the Enclave Economy Thesis: Chinese Immigrants in the Ethnic Labor Market." *Amerasia* 17: 5–21.

Model, Suzanne. 1985. "A Comparative Perspective on the Ethnic Enclave: Blacks, Italians, and Jews in New York City." *International Migration Review* 19: 64–81.

———. 1992. "The Ethnic Economy: Cubans and Chinese Reconsidered." *Sociological Quarterly* 33: 63–82.

Modell, John. 1977. *The Economics and Politics of Racial Accommodation.* Urbana: University of Illinois Press.

Nee, Victor, and Jimy M. Sanders. 1987. "On Testing the Enclave-Economy Hypothesis." *American Sociological Review* 52: 771–73.

Oliver, Melvin L., and Thomas M. Shapiro. 1990. "Wealth of a Nation." *American Journal of Economics and Sociology* 49: 129–50.

Perez, Lisandro. 1986. "Immigrant Economic Adjustment and Family Organization: The Cuban Success Story Reexamined." *International Migration Review* 20: 4–20.

Portes, Alejandro. 1981. "Mode of Incorporation and Theories of Labor Immigration." In *Global Trends in Migration,* edited by Mary Kritz, Charles B. Keeley, and Silvano Tomasi. New York: Center for Migration Studies.

Portes, Alejandro, and Robert Bach. 1985. *Latin Journey: Cuban and Mexican Immigrants in the United States.* Berkeley: University of California Press.

Portes, Alejandro, and Leif Jensen. 1987. "What's an Ethnic Enclave? The Case for Conceptual Clarity." *American Sociological Review* 52: 768–71.

——. 1989. "The Enclave and the Entrants: Patterns of Ethnic Enterprise in Miami before and after Mariel." *American Sociological Review* 54: 929–49.

Portes, Alejandro, and Robert D. Manning. 1986. "The Immigrant Enclave: Theory and Empirical Examples." In *Comparative Ethnic Relations*, edited by Susan Olzak and Joane Nagel. New York: Academic Press.

Reitz, Jeffrey. 1980. *The Survival of Ethnic Groups*. Toronto: McGraw-Hill.

Sakamoto, Arthur, and Meichu D. Chen. 1991. "Inequality and Attainment in a Dual Labor Market." *American Sociological Review* 56: 295–308.

Sanders, Jimy M., and Victor Nee. 1987. "Limits of Ethnic Solidarity." *American Sociological Review* 52: 745–67.

Sullivan, Teresa A. 1981. "Sociological Views of Labor Markets: Some Missed Opportunities and Neglected Dimensions." Chap. 12 in *Sociological Perspectives on Labor Markets*, edited by Ivar Berg. New York: Academic Press.

Tolbert, Charles, Patrick M. Horan, and E. M. Beck. 1980. "The Structure of Economic Segmentation." *American Journal of Sociology* 85: 1095–116.

U.S. Department of Commerce. 1988. Bureau of Labor Statistics. *Labor Force Statistics Derived from the Current Population Survey, 1948–87*. Bulletin 2307. Washington, D.C.: U.S. Government Printing Office.

——. 1991. Bureau of the Census. *1987 Economic Censuses*. MB87-4. *Survey of Minority-Owned Business Enterprises, Summary*. Washington, D.C.: U.S. Government Printing Office.

Wacquant, Loic. In press. "Redrawing the Urban Color Line: The State of the Ghetto in the 1980s." In *Social Problems*, edited by Craig Calhoun and George Ritzer. New York: McGraw-Hill.

Ward, Robin. 1987. "Resistance, Accommodation, and Advantage: Strategic Development of Ethnic Business." In *The Manufacture of Disadvantage*, edited by Gloria Lee and Ray Loveridge. Milton Keynes, England: Open University Press.

Wilson, Kenneth L., and W. Allen Martin. 1982. "Ethnic Enclaves: A Comparison of the Cuban and Black Economies." *American Journal of Sociology* 88: 135–60.

Wilson, Kenneth L., and Alejandro Portes. 1980. "Immigrant Enclaves: An Analysis of the Labor Market Experiences of Cubans in Miami." *American Journal of Sociology* 86: 305–19.

Wong, Bernard. 1987. "The Role of Ethnicity in Enclave Enterprises: A Study of the Chinese Garment Factories in New York City." *Human Organization* 46: 120–30.

Yoon, Cheong-Ok. 1992. "The Information Seeking Behavior of Koreans in the United States." Ph.D. diss., University of California, Los Angeles.

Zenner, Walter. 1991. *Minorities in the Middle*. Albany: State University of New York Press.

Zentgraf, Kristine M. 1989. "Gender, Immigration, and Economic Restructuring in Los Angeles." *California Sociologist* 12: 111–36.

Zhou, Min, and John Logan. 1989. "Returns on Human Capital in Ethnic Enclaves." *American Sociological Review* 54: 809–20.

Chapter 3

Ethnicity
and the Entrepreneur:
Self-Employment among
Former Soviet Jewish Refugees

Marilyn Halter

In an essay entitled "Soviet Jewish Emigres in the U.S.—What We Know and What We Don't Know," Steven Gold, author of *Refugee Communities: A Comparative Field Study,* put knowledge of the phenomenon of self-employment squarely in the Don't Know column, encouraging future researchers to give attention to Soviet Jewish entrepreneurs (Gold 1991). He also noted that these immigrant businesses are of particular significance because of the historic role of the self-employed in fostering ethnic community formation.[1]

The relative paucity of studies of Soviet Jewish refugees in general is surprising, given the wealth of scholarship on other aspects of the history of Jewish migration flows, as well as studies devoted to the meaning of Jewish ethnicity. The example of the former Soviet Jews in business should be of particular interest given how key the Jewish experience has been to our understanding of ethnic enterprise. From Werner Sombart's linkage of Jewish entrepreneurship with religious ideas found in Judaism to the term "Jewmaicans" used to name the successfully self-employed West Indians in New York City, the Jewish proprietor has always been the quintessential ethnic entrepreneur (Sombart 1951).

The phenomenon of self-employment among Soviet Jewish émigrés as viewed in comparative perspective offers an interesting and, at times, perplexing case study. Without benefit of prior experience in a free market economy, they have, relative to the other populations in the Boston project, done very well in their business ventures. Russian Jews, both the second wave at the turn of the century and the recent migrants, demonstrate a continuity of business success—despite coming from radically differing political systems and despite engaging in different strategies for action once they arrived in the United States. Jewish immigrant entrepreneurs have undergone a shift in this century away from dependence on collective resources and a well-developed associational life (especially in the form of the Hebrew Free Loan and *landsmanschaften* organizations) toward highly individualistic and informal strategies for economic development. Among the recent émigrés, their premigration circumstances afforded them little experience with entrepreneurship and their modis operandi once here is a departure from the strategies of earlier generations of coethnics. But like those before them, they succeed. And their perception of that achievement is intricately bound up with a sense of Jewishness.

The findings of the Boston research reveal several distinct aspects of Soviet Jewish economic culture that have converged to facilitate their adaptation to a capitalist system and that help explain their relative success in small business endeavors. These factors include the bonds of trust that have been transplanted to the U.S. immigrant community, the role of women in entrepreneurship, the position of Soviet Jews as twice minorities, and the belief in entrepreneurial propensity as inherent to their ethnicity.

Characteristics of the Boston Soviet Jewish Business Community

Between 1965 and 1993, more than 270,000 Jews from the former Soviet Union migrated to the United States. Since 1988, their numbers have steadily increased, reaching a high in 1992 of 45,303 in a single year; the increased numbers have made settlers from the Soviet Union the largest group of refugees to enter the United States. In 1990, Soviet refugees surpassed the number of Southeast Asian refugee arrivals to the state of Massachusetts. However, more than half the newcomers from the former Soviet Union live in either New York or California, settling in the New York City area and Los Angeles county; only 5 percent of the total influx reside in Massachusetts. A precise count of the number of Soviet Jewish business owners in the Greater Boston area cannot be made, but the universe is comparatively small, approximately 5 percent of the ten thousand Russian Jewish immigrants to the area (HIAS 1993; Chiswick 1993, 262–64).[2]

Most of the migrants came to Boston seeking professional employment. Arriving in this country with high levels of education and extensive technical training, they were drawn in the late 1970s and early 1980s to Boston at the onset of the Massachusetts Miracle. A psychological study of Soviet Jewish refugees who settled in Boston between 1973 and 1982 found that engineers and other professionals with technical backgrounds readily found work in the area. Furthermore, because of the largely technical component of their occupations, fluent English was not required. They were able to obtain jobs in their fields immediately upon arrival by using their existing premigration training and skills. Thus, the process of resettlement was fairly easily accomplished, at least in the critical arena of employment (Sales 1984).

With its wealth of institutions of higher learning, Boston also attracted members of the intelligentsia. The collective self-image of the Boston Russian Jewish community as highly cultured and professionally trained resists identification with business activity. One of the first things my primary contact in the community said to me upon hearing about the project was, "Why are you doing entrepreneurs. It's so easy. Everyone thinks of Soviet Jews as entrepreneurs. It's a stereotype and they know it."[3]

Other cities with larger concentrations of Soviet Jewish immigrants, such as New York and Los Angeles, have higher rates of entrepreneurship than does Boston.[4] Moreover, all the businesses in Boston are small-scale establishments, with few or no employees, sole or family proprietorship, and simple storefront facilities. Soviet Jewish communities in New York, Los Angeles, and Chicago boast larger firms with more elaborate operations, as well as competing shops providing the same types of goods or services. However, because the refugees have been resettled throughout the United States, there are no large-scale Soviet Jewish urban enclaves comparable to the dense concentrations of such well-developed ethnic communities as the Cubans in Miami or the Koreans in Los Angeles. The closest to an ethnic enclave of this type among the Soviet Jews is Brooklyn's Brighton Beach settlement.[5]

Although the number of Soviet Jewish businesses in Boston is small, it is a growing sector of the economy. The *Boston Russian Bulletin*, a monthly advertising circular, tripled in size during the course of this research. New enterprises appeared in the ads each month, and it was not uncommon to hear from various sources in the community of a new Russian Jewish business opening its doors. (The cover letter to potential advertisers that accompanies the *Russian Bulletin*, however, downplays its use as a vehicle for business advertising, emphasizing instead its promise as a forum for announcements of educational opportunities, professional employment, and cultural events.) In 1993, the Jewish Vocational Service launched the Microenterprise Training and Loan Program for Refugees to assist newcomers in starting up small businesses. The program offers courses on how a free market economy works and practical skills training that introduces the students to such critical concepts of small business operation as recordkeeping, market research, cash-flow projections, and workman's compensation. Equally important has been a grant from the Office of Refugee Resettlement for making small loans available to the program's participants. Within a few months, refugees had already benefited from the technical assistance and the loan program to open up a sprinkling of new ventures. The steady start-up of small businesses, in general, may well reflect the shrinking opportunities in the professional and technical occupational categories in Massachusetts since the mid-1980s.

All the respondents in this study have resided in Boston for at least five years, and all left Russia as adults with refugee status, arriving in the United States between 1975 and 1986. This period is considered to be the first wave of recent Soviet Jewish migration, with most coming to this country between 1975 and 1980. Newcomers from 1987 to 1993 constitute the second wave.[6]

Although migrants may offer political or religious reasons for emigrating, all mentioned economic motives as well. In several instances entrepreneurs made no pretense of having emigrated for any reason other than an economic one. Some spoke of abortive attempts to conduct business under the Soviet regime, when they lived in constant fear of being discovered for engaging in black-market activity. One interviewee whose Boston store had been robbed and who narrowly escaped being mugged in the process, nonetheless maintained that the fear of everyday street crime in the United States was preferable to the daily terror of repression he experienced in the former USSR. For some, the best part of being in this country has been to freely engage in entrepreneurial activities without the risk of political reprisal.

Steven Gold (1992, 179–83) argued that refugees are at a disadvantage, compared to voluntary migrants, because of the amount of capital they carry into this country. He stressed that Soviet refugees were severely restricted in this way and arrived with few assets. Gold further described the difficulty of maintaining business connections with compatriots in their native country because these connections had to be severed. Boston Soviet Jewish entrepreneurs, however, generally found ways of bringing in larger amounts of capital, operating in the black-market, and using ingenuity and family and community ties to accumulate initial capital in order to make the move. Several came with substantial resources and are comparatively well off. They developed an elaborate, under-the-table system of accumulating capital and transferring resources to this country. Moreover, since the demise of the socialist regime, although they still arrive with refugee status, many are taking advantage of relaxed laws to establish joint ventures, keeping up business ties and traveling back and forth in order to maintain a trading relationship with business partners in Russia.

An Ethnic Web Economy

Historically, Jewish immigrant businesses in Boston were more spatially concentrated, flourishing along Blue Hill Avenue, the central artery of the inner city's contiguous Jewish residential neighborhoods. The district was a classic example of a bustling ethnic enclave where the economic, social, political, religious, and family life of the community intersected in a clearly defined geographic area. Today, no such dynamic Jewish enclave exists in the city, although neighborhoods with higher concentrations of Jewish American residents can be found in some parts of the Greater Boston area, such as Brookline, Newton, and Lynn. Russian Jewish refugees no longer find a well-defined ethnic community, and the newest Jewish arrivals are settling in a more scattered pattern. When they start up a business, they may try to locate it in a shopping district adjacent to an area with larger numbers of Jewish residents, but they are just as likely to end up situated in a mixed neighborhood.

The spatial configuration of ethnic enterprises has often proved to be a significant factor in successfully maintaining and operating immigrant businesses. This is particularly true when a well-developed and vigorous ethnic enclave already exists or the businesses are aggregated in one central location amid coethnic residents.[7] Neither model obtains for the Soviet Jewish entrepreneurs in Boston, yet geographic dispersion has not been the sole determinant of the level of ethnic community they have experienced. Despite their relative spatial isolation, Russian Jewish businesses are still linked to each other and to the larger coethnic community—connected in a lattice of economic, social, and familial bonds that I have termed an ethnic web economy. Although more spread out spatially than an ethnic enclave or neighborhood, the businesses exhibit a degree of informal interdependence that gives the web its coherence and shape. For example, these ethnic networks provide essential start-up capital and other financial support to new businesses and furnish a ready pool of potential employees. The social and informational links in the web are invaluable in fostering ethnic community.

Apart from one or two grocery stores and restaurants, the Russian Jewish enterprises do not target a solely coethnic clientele. Even the more ethnic establishments want to appeal to the non-ethnic community, and services are directed to the general population. Typically, customers are not Russian Jews, although they may be American Jews. Most owners want to be successful beyond the coethnic community, and several stated that they prefer non–Russian Jewish customers. Some of the businesses are situated in the most upscale commercial areas of Boston and Cambridge, districts set apart from ethnic residential neighborhoods.

Some shops, nevertheless, do specialize in ethnic products appealing to a coethnic clientele, and when attempts are made to Americanize business practices the owners may meet resistance from their customers. Such was the case with the proprietor of a Russian grocery store and deli who had studied at an American business school and whose store was frequented by both Soviet Jewish refugees and native-born Americans. She made a conscious effort to modify her marketing procedures, modernize operations, and put into practice some of what she had learned about the American approach. For the most part, her initiatives backfired. As she became more efficient at serving her customers so they would not have to stand in line, many Soviet Jewish patrons complained; some stopped shopping there altogether. Long lines had been a sign to them of a thriving business that sold goods worth waiting for. If there was no wait, then they reasoned that the products were not fresh or there was something wrong with them. For similar reasons, the owner rarely put items on sale. Bargain prices were equated with inferior quality. What was meant to reflect improved service was interpreted by the immigrants as an indication that the business was not doing well. Certainly the owner did not want to convey this impression to a sizable portion of her customers, so she went back to the more familiar way of conducting business. The clash of cultures played itself out in this attempt to adapt to a Russian Jewish–*American* business environment.

Intragroup Differences

Ongoing research on the Iranian ethnic economy in Los Angeles has de-lineated the various ethnic subgroups that constitute the Iranian immi-grant community. The phenomenon of internal ethnicity has received slight attention in the ethnic enterprise literature, but as the preliminary findings concerning Iranian self-employment indicate, differences be-tween the four ethnoreligious subgroups—Armenians, Bahais, Jews, and Muslims—go a long way toward explaining the socioeconomic dynamics of this highly entrepreneurial population (Light et al. 1993). Similarly, Russian Jewish immigrant entrepreneurs in Boston exhibit internal eth-nicity and can be broken down into two distinct types. The first group are those who migrated in the initial wave (1975–86). They were trained and worked in various occupations in Russia and took up business only upon arrival in this country. They have been called the more Russian Russians. More recent arrivals, who hail primarily from the Ukrainian city of Odessa, had experience with the free market and the loosening of state controls prior to emigration. They were entrepreneurs in the former Soviet Union and are entrepreneurs in America. These are the hustlers, characterized as wheeling-dealing go-getters, full of energy and with a boundless zeal for involvement in business. They all seem to know each other, had similar levels of training as coordinators in the Ukraine, and form a loose network of association along the East Coast.[8]

These distinctions within the business sector reflect similar intra-group divisions among the larger Russian Jewish population. Length of time in this country, regional origins, social class, and residential pat-terns all stratify the Greater Boston ethnic community. Those who ar-rived in the first wave generally emigrated from Moscow or Leningrad. They were professionally trained and highly educated. Their motives for migrating were more political and religious than economic, and many have settled in the middle-class Boston neighborhood of Brookline. The more recent émigrés, predominantly from the Ukraine, arrived in the United States with technological training or craft skills. At the time of their arrival they could not afford Boston housing prices and often set-tled in outlying areas, such as Lynn or Revere. Typically, they emigrated for more clearly economic reasons.

The two groups socialize in different circles, and it is not uncommon to hear pejorative remarks made by one about the other. The highly educated Moscovites consider themselves more cosmopolitan, looking down upon the boorish Ukrainians, whereas those from Odessa consider the Russian Russians as pretentious and inept at adapting to the American social system. One observer remarked that the longer the migrants are in this country, the more pronounced are these divisions.

This reverses the classic pattern of U.S. immigrants who, initially are fragmented along local, religious, or linguistic lines, and later evolve into nationally identified ethnic groups as they adapt to American society. This model has been most systematically documented in the case of Italian-American identity formation. Among new arrivals from Italy at the turn of the century, primary loyalty was given to one's village or region. Thus, the migrants defined themselves first as Sicilians or Neapolitans. However, in the process of adapting to their new environment, they invented a national, or Italian-American, identity that superseded local allegiances.[9]

All such sources of ethnic identification, whether internal to a subgroup or placed on the larger ethnic configuration, stem from boundaries created through bonds of trust and facility of communication. Unlike the evolution of Italian ethnicity from a fragmented to a more unified entity earlier in the century, recent Russian Jewish arrivals reported an opposite trend. While living in the USSR, as long as you were against the state, a sense of solidarity and group cohesion existed. Internal schisms receded into the background in the face of the unifying effect of antigovernment sentiment. This was community in opposition. Once resettled in the United States, the harmony disappeared as different opinions were openly expressed, a more critical stance could be taken, and intragroup distinctions became more evident.

Soviet Jewish Economic Culture

Bonds of Trust

Boston Soviet Jewish entrepreneurs demonstrate high levels of individualism. Most belong to no formal organizations, clubs, or voluntary groups, nor to fraternal, synagogue, or small business associations. They explain their lack of involvement by referring to premigration circumstances where they felt bureaucratized and claustrophobic because of governmentally enforced collectivism and extremely crowded living conditions. Thus, they now spurn affiliations in both the domestic and the public spheres. Respondents expressed skepticism and cynicism about formal association life, preferring, instead, to carve out individual space and work toward self-sufficiency.

This antigroup behavior does not extend to small circles of close friends and family however. These are informal networks of internal ethnicity—what anthropologist Fran Markowitz called "community without organizations" (1993, 225). Within this small relational configuration, one can find sources of capital. People readily borrow from one another with no formal contractual agreements. Even when the sum is sizable, this type of lending is done with few questions asked and with confidence that the loan will be repaid and the favor returned, if needed. This pattern replicates a similar one practiced in the Soviet Union, where the strategy for living with government-sanctioned intervention into the private arena led the Jewish population to rely on a handful of trusted friends. Part of the obligation of these sacred friendships was to readily give financial assistance.

These bonds of trust among family members and friends have been re-created in the United States and are crucial to the successful economic adaptation of the new émigrés. For immigrants without investment capital or collateral and without secure credit histories, relying on formal lending institutions is not an option. Nor do the Soviet Jews bring with them a tradition of rotating credit associations, although the long-standing Jewish American Hebrew Free Loan associations still operate in some areas of this country and have been known, on occasion, to give loans to Soviet Jewish refugees (Tenenbaum 1992). One reason the informal system works as well as it does is that enough individuals in the émigré community have been able to reach higher income levels, which enable them to provide for those who are still struggling. But results of the Boston research indicate that the longer an immigrant lives in the United States, the more likely the enduring and reciprocal nature of these integrated networks is to shift. As one interviewee stated, "In Russia, if you need money, you can't borrow from the bank, one kopeck. You borrow money from friends. Here, in a year, two, or three, we become Americans. We smile one to another and ask hello, how are you. If someone asks me now for money, I'll say, please, go to the bank." He then gave a smile himself and declared, "Now I am American."

Role of Women

Further contributing to the successful adaptation of Russian Jewish immigrants is the role of women in business. The gender composition of the Soviet Jewish entrepreneurs in Boston is unique: almost half the businesses are owned by women. In the typical immigrant enterprise, the male head of household is the owner; his wife (and, at times, the older children) assist in running the business, thus relying on traditional gender roles of the family economy to facilitate successful operation of the venture. Particularly in the crucial start-up phase, the wives, who are unpaid, often provide a variety of services such as cashiering or keeping the books. Many continue to act as a reserve labor force throughout the life of the business. When women do appear as the sole proprietors of a business, they are almost always engaged in enterprises within the customary female domain, such as child care or beauty and skin care services. Immigrant women who are self-employed are also more likely to be unmarried, whether widowed or divorced.[10]

The ownership patterns of Soviet Jewish businesses in Boston depart from this norm. Female entrepreneurs were found in a variety of enterprises including furniture, clothing, gift shops, restaurants, and grocery stores, as well as the more common categories of beauty and skin care salons, child care services, and bridal shops. Most of the female owners were married, and their spouses worked in the larger economy, some as professionals, others in the service sector. In a few cases, the husband also ran a separate business, and in more than one instance the gender roles of the standard family business were reversed. The husband of one proprietor of a skin care salon did all the bookkeeping for her; an exclusive gift shop owner's spouse, who was himself employed as a music teacher, came to the store after his work was done to assist his wife as a salesclerk. Instances of unrelated female co-ownership of a single business were found exclusively among the Soviet Jewish entrepreneurs in this study, as was the only case of a mother and daughter coproprietorship. And in one co-ownership arrangement, the business partner of the female proprietor of a thriving venture is an unrelated male. Both partners in this business are married.

Thus, unlike other immigrant populations, the gender differences in entrepreneurship among Soviet Jews are minimal. Women operate as independent owners in a range of businesses and enter into partnerships with equal and full involvement. The female émigrés came from an environment where women, whether married or single, worked alongside men as full participants in the labor force. They arrived in the United States with job skills and training, accustomed to working outside the home and ready to fulfill egalitarian gender role expectations that were consistent with their premigration socialization.

Such conditions have probably made the transition to the United States less stressful on the Soviet Jewish family, overall, than it has been for other recent immigrant groups who come from native countries that are much more patriarchal in structure. Several studies have demonstrated that the process of migration can upset the gender role balance both inside and outside the home, particularly when the woman takes an active economic role and achieves financial independence. Research on the Dominican immigrant household, for example, has shown that domestic tensions were exacerbated by a shift in gender relations. With women typically working for wages outside the household in the United States, the traditional patriarchal structure, where the male is the sole income provider and the female remains at home providing child care and other domestic services, is seriously challenged. This familial role restructuring often generates increased levels of stress between husband and wife, conflict that if unresolved, leads to higher rates of marital instability, including separation and divorce (Grasmuck and Pessar 1991, 156–61). Similar evidence of heightened antagonism between husband and wife over the struggle to create a more egalitarian household was found among Haitian immigrants in New York and Vietnamese refugees in Philadelphia (Stafford, in Foner 1987, 131–54; Kibria 1993).

The process of adaptation can create many varieties of stress and turmoil. Recent Soviet Jewish migrants appear to be exempt from the particular and often intensive strain of having to renegotiate gender roles within the family economy. Furthermore, for the Soviet Jewish entrepreneurial families where one spouse is successfully self-employed while the other works full-time at a separate career, or where both are self-employed, the dual income increases the likelihood of steady upward mobility.

Twice Minorities

The minority position that recent Soviet Jewish refugees hold in the United States is not new to them. Unlike their Greek counterparts, the ethnic group that is most akin to them in rates of entrepreneurial participation and success, Russian Jews were not the dominant nationality in their country of origin. On the contrary, their experience in the Soviet Union reflected a generations-old legacy of European and Russian anti-Semitism. Their Jewishness elicited inferior treatment and state-sanctioned hostility and discrimination. Limits were placed on the extent to which they could hold power in government and its extended bureaucracy, as well as on their access to higher professional education and technical training in the USSR.

Forced to find alternative ways to make a decent life for themselves, the Soviet Jewish respondents expressed pride in their ability to manipulate the system and to make do. Consequently, when the immigrants arrived in the United States still in a position of disadvantage (whether because they were unable to speak the language, lacked financial resources, or were simply not familiar with American society) they found themselves in a familiar role. When confronted with the challenge of operating at a disadvantage under new circumstances, their history of living as an oppressed minority gave them an edge. Several studies of immigrant populations that can be categorized as twice minorities, including Jews at other times and places, corroborate the potential economic and political advantages of having built a community infrastructure as a survival strategy in response to persecution.[11]

In terms of daily life and regional variation in the USSR, anti-Semitism was most pervasive in the provincial areas such as the Ukraine. Some Jewish residents of the major Russian cities, although never allowed to fully assimilate into Soviet society, did find ingenious ways of working their way into the more elite strata and were able to participate in many aspects of the cultural life. When they emigrate to the United States, they are much less likely than their Ukrainian counterparts to go into business. For Soviet Jewish émigrés with refusenik status, the population had already risked everything from losing jobs and being thrown out of universities to arrest and forced relocations—to make the move. Here was a self-selected group already predisposed to taking risks. Once they left, their Soviet citizenship would be revoked. Not surprisingly, these political refugees, having already taken the risk of emigrating from the Soviet Union, are then willing to take the risk of going into business.

Belief in Entrepreneurial Propensity

Among the Jewish entrepreneurs from the former Soviet Union interviewed for this study, there existed a shared sense of the historical role of the Jewish people as disadvantaged—a role they have countered by going into business. The legacy of this positioning within the social structure has been incorporated into the cultural ethos of this group. The concept of the Jew as survivor has been internalized by the Soviet Jewish immigrants, becoming part of the cultural makeup that may either motivate or explain the decision to start a business in this country.

They have transformed their situational role into a cultural characteristic. Recent statistical findings relating ethnicity with entrepreneurship in the United States point to a positive correlation between belief in one's ability to succeed at business and the likelihood of successfully engaging in such an endeavor (Butler and Herring 1991, 91). The legacy of a strong self-employment tradition among global Jewry fuels the entrepreneurial efforts of Russian Jews who have had little experience with free enterprise in their lifetimes. The respondents in this study made definitive connections between their Jewish background and their business acumen. They described how they needed to be ingenious and to craftily manipulate the environment in order to survive in the former Soviet Union. It was their Jewishness that enabled these strategies.

By viewing entrepreneurial know-how as an inborn character trait, they have constructed a collective identity that relates their Jewish ethnicity to business success. It becomes, in a sense, a self-fulfilling prophecy. In addition to their alleged instinctive skill in business, émigrés claim that hard work and resiliency are cultural attributes that predispose them toward entrepreneurship. Russian Jewish entrepreneurs are roughly equating Jewish ethnicity with a petit bourgeois-class position. Their self-defined ethnicity was obviously incompatible with the Soviet system's collectivism and ban on private property. They were, in fact, frustrated capitalists who are now flourishing in the new economic environment. As one owner put it, "If you are Jewish, you know how to survive. We are drilled to survive. We're drilled to deal with bureaucracy. We know how to be tough. It's a part of us. It's in our blood." In some respects, Boston's Soviet Jewish migrants have an advantage when compared to other recent immigrant populations. Nevertheless, many of the respondents in this study saw themselves as having gone into business simply because that is what Jews have always done in response to anti-Semitism and economic closure. Even when the opportunity structure is favorable, they identify Jewishness as being without equal access to these opportunities. The explanation for Soviet Jewish entrepreneurial activity represents an amalgam of cultural, historical, and structural factors intricately woven together.

Notes

1. Throughout this chapter the terms "Soviet Jews" and "Russian Jews" are used interchangeably to refer to Jewish refugees from the former USSR, whether they emigrated before or after the dissolution of the Soviet Union and whether they

originated from Russia itself or from the Ukraine, unless these distinctions are specifically noted in the text.

2. Figures for Massachusetts and the Boston Metropolitan area are based on the 1990 census (weighted 5 percent Public Use Microdata Sample). Census data are based on nationality, not religion, thus there is no way to know precisely how many of the migrants from the USSR are Jewish. However, particularly up until 1990, other calculations (Chiswick 1993; HIAS 1993; Gold 1993) corroborate that a very high proportion of refugees from the former Soviet Union are Jewish. Since 1990, non-Jewish migrants from the former USSR have been relocating to the United States in increasing numbers.

3. I am enormously indebted to Pearl Morgovsky for her resourceful, energetic, and insightful research assistance on this project. Vivien Goldman also conducted several interviews.

4. Data from the 1990 census show that in New York, 15 percent were self-employed (21 percent of men and 8 percent of women) while for Los Angeles the figure jumps to an astounding 24 percent (31 percent of men and 13 percent of women). Because Los Angeles is also the hub of settlement for many of the Soviet Armenian immigrants, who are also highly entrepreneurial, it must be assumed that the high rates of self-employment reflect both Jewish and non-Jewish Soviet immigrant participation (see Gold forthcoming, tables 19 and 20).

5. For discussions of Soviet Jewish businesses in other locales, see Annilese Orleck, "The Soviet Jews: Life in Brighton Beach, Brooklyn," in Foner 1987, 273–304, and Gold 1988b, 411–38.

6. Respondents were contacted through snowball sampling. Businesses represented included restaurants, grocery, deli and candy stores, beauty and skin care salons, shoemakers, publishing, insurance, dry cleaning, alterations, child care, ballet and art schools, clothing, bridal, furniture, and jewelry stores, gift shops, travel agencies, taxi, auto body and electronics repair.

7. See, for example, Portes and Bach 1985; Model 1985; Golab 1977.

8. As of this writing, informal conversations with some who have emigrated to New York City very recently (since Perestroika) reveal a new pattern of entrepreneurship developing. These individuals tend to be involved in illegal joint ventures with large amounts of money and profit changing hands. This is an all male network of émigrés again primarily from Odessa working through a configuration of family and regional connections whose business schemes, organization and general disregard for international law in their ventures has led one respondent to compare them to the Italian mafia.

9. See Barton 1975; Dinnerstein and Reimers 1975; Vecoli 1983.

10. See, for example, Bonacich and Modell 1981, 187–95; Sasha Josephides, "Honour, Family, and Work: Greek Cypriot Women before and after Migration," in Westwood and Bhachu 1988, 24–57; Moallem 1991; Portes and Stepick 1993, 128.

11. See Espiritu 1989; Bhachu 1985; Viviani 1984, 259–65; Hendricks 1923.

References

Barton, Josef. 1975. *Peasants and Strangers*. Cambridge: Harvard University Press.

Berman, Igor. 1979. "Soviet Jews and Emigration." *Soviet Jewish Affairs* 9: 46–63.

Bhachu, Parminder. 1985. *Twice Migrants: East African Sikh Settlers in Britain*. London: Tavistock.

Bonacich, Edna, and John Modell. 1981. *The Economic Basis of Ethnic Solidarity: A Study of Japanese Americans.* Berkeley: University of California Press.

Butler, John Sibley, and Cedric Herring. 1991. "Ethnicity and Entrepreneurship in America: Toward an Explanation of Racial and Ethnic Group Variations in Self-Employment." *Sociological Perspectives* 34, no. 1: 79–94.

Chiswick, Barry. 1993. "Soviet Jews in the United States: An Analysis of Their Linguistic and Economic Adjustment." *International Migration Review* 27, no. 102.

Dinnerstein, Leonard, and David Reimers. 1975. *Ethnic Americans.* New York: Dodd and Mead.

Espiritu, Yen Le. 1989. "Beyond the 'Boat People': Ethnicization of American Life." *Amerasia* 15, no. 2: 49–67.

Foner, Nancy, ed. 1987. *New Immigrants in New York.* New York: Columbia University Press.

Freedman, Robert O., ed. 1984. *Soviet Jewry in the Decisive Decade, 1971–1980.* Durham, N.C.: Duke University Press.

——. 1989. *Soviet Jewry in the 1980s: The Politics of Anti-Semitism and Emigration and the Dynamics of Resettlement.* Durham, N.C.: Duke University Press.

Gitelman, Zvi. 1982. "Soviet Immigrant Resettlement in the United States." *Soviet Jewish Affairs* 12, no. 2: 3–18.

Golab, Caroline. 1977. *Immigrant Destinations.* Philadelphia: Temple University Press.

Gold, Steven J. 1988a. "Patterns of Interaction and Adjustment among Soviet Jewish Refugees: Findings from an Ethnography in the San Francisco Bay Area." *Contemporary Jewry* 9, no. 2: 87–105.

——. 1988b. "Refugees and Small Business: The Case of Soviet Jews and Vietnamese." *Ethnic and Racial Studies* 11, no. 4: 411–38.

——. 1991. "Soviet Jews in the U.S.: What We Know and What We Don't Know." Paper presented at Wilstein Institute Conference on Soviet Jews in the United States, Stanford University, June.

——. 1992. *Refugee Communities: A Comparative Field Study.* Newbury Park, Calif.: Sage Publications.

——. 1994. "Soviet Jews in the United States." *American Jewish Year Book:* 3–57.

Goldstein, Ed. 1979. "Psychological Adaption of Soviet Immigrants." *American Journal of Psychoanalysis* 39: 257–63.

Grasmuck, Sherri, and Patricia R. Pessar. 1991. *Between Two Islands: Dominican International Migration.* Berkeley: University of California Press.

Hendricks, Burton J. 1923. *The Jews in America.* New York: Doubleday, Page.

HIAS. 1993. "Annual Statistics 1965–1993."

Jacobs, Don N., and Ellen Frankel Paul. 1981. *Studies of the Third Wave: Recent Migration of Soviet Jews to the United States.* Boulder, Colo.: Westview Press.

Kessner, Thomas, and Betty Caroli. 1986. *Today's Immigrants: Their Stories.* New York: Oxford University Press.

Kibria, Nazli. 1993. *Family Tightrope: The Changing Lives of Vietnamese Americans.* Princeton, N.J.: Princeton University Press.

Kosmin, Barry. 1990. *The Class of 1979: The "Acculturation" of Jewish Immigrants from the Soviet Union.* New York: Council of Jewish Federations.

Light, Ivan, and Edna Bonacich. 1988. *Immigrant Entrepreneurs: Koreans in Los Angeles, 1965–1982.* Berkeley: University of California Press.

Light, Ivan, Georges Sabagh, Mehdi Bozorgmehr, and Claudia Der-Martirosian.

1993. "Internal Ethnicity in the Ethnic Economy." *Ethnic and Racial Studies* 16, no. 4: 581–97.

Markowitz, Fran. 1988a. "Rituals as Keys to Soviet Immigrants' Jewish Identity." In *Between Two Worlds: Ethnographic Essays on American Jewry*, edited by Jack Kugelmass. Ithaca, N.Y.: Cornell University Press.

——. 1988b. "Jewish in the USSR, Russian in the USA." In *Persistence and Flexibility: Anthropological Perspectives on the American Jewish Experience*, edited by Walter P. Zenner. Albany: State University of New York Press.

——. 1993. *A Community in Spite of Itself: Soviet Jewish Émigrés in New York*. Washington: Smithsonian Institution Press.

Moallem, Minoo. 1991. "Gender, Ethnicity and Entrepreneurship." Paper presented at the annual meeting of the American Sociological Association. Cincinnati, Ohio, August.

Model, Suzanne. 1985. "A Comparative Perspective on the Ethnic Enclave: Blacks, Italians, and Jews in New York City." *International Migration Review* 19, no. 1: 64–81.

Office of Refugee Resettlement. 1986. *Report to Congress: Refugee Resettlement Program*.

Office for Refugees and Immigrants of the Commonwealth of Massachusetts. 1990. "Social Need Survey of Immigrants to the North Shore from the Soviet Union." Salem, Mass.: Jewish Family Service of the North Shore, June.

Portes, Alejandro, and Robert Bach. 1985. *Latin Journey: Cuban and Mexican Immigrants in the United States*. Berkeley: University of California Press.

Portes, Alejandro, and Alex Stepick. 1993. *City on the Edge: The Transformation of Miami*. Berkeley: University of California Press.

Ripp, Victor. 1984. *From Moscow to Main Street: Among the Russian Émigrés*. Boston: Little, Brown.

Rothchild, Sylvia. 1985. *A Special Legacy: An Oral History of Soviet Jewish Émigrés in the United States*. New York: Simon and Schuster.

Sales, Amy L. 1984. "Patterns of Community Contact and Immigrant Adjustment: A Study of the Soviet Jews in Boston." Ph.D. diss. Boston University.

Simon, Rita. 1985a. "Soviet Jews." In *Refugees in the United States: A Reference Handbook*, edited by David W. Haines. Westport, Conn.: Greenwood Press.

——, ed. 1985b. *New Lives: The Adjustment of Soviet Jewish Immigrants to the United States and Israel*. Lexington, Mass.: D. C. Heath, Lexington Books.

Simon, Rita, Louise Shelley, and Paul Schneiderman. 1986. "The Social and Economic Adjustment of Soviet Jewish Women in the United States." In *International Migration: The Female Experience*, edited by Rita Simon and Caroline Brettell. Totowa, N.J.: Rowan and Allanheld.

Sombart, Werner. 1951. *The Jews and Modern Capitalism*. Glencoe, Ill.: Free Press.

Stack, John F. 1979. *International Conflict in an American City: Boston's Irish, Italians, and Jews, 1935–1944*. Westport, Conn.: Greenwood Press.

Tenenbaum, Shelly. 1992. Conversation with the author, 1 May.

Vecoli, Rudolf. 1983. "The Formation of Chicago's Little Italies." *Journal of American Ethnic History* 2: 5–20.

Viviani, Nancy. 1984. *The Long Journey: Vietnamese Migration and Settlement in Australia*. Carlton, Vic.: Melbourne University Press.

Westwood, Sallie, and Parminder Bhachu. 1988. *Enterprising Women: Ethnicity, Gender, and Gender Relations*. London: Routledge.

Chapter 4

Culture, Economic Stability, and Entrepreneurship: The Case of British West Indians in Boston

Violet Johnson

By the end of the first half of the twentieth century, West Indian immigrants, thanks mainly to propaganda by West Indian writers and activists, were being touted for their phenomenal success in small business enterprise in America.[1] This view first gained scholarly prominence with the publication in 1912 of Edmund Haynes's study *The Negro at Work in New York*. In this volume, Haynes showed that whereas West Indian immigrants constituted only about 9 percent of the total black population of New York City, they owned almost 20 percent of the black businesses (Haynes 1912, 101–2). The uncritical acceptance of this pioneering work has contributed immensely to the perpetuation of the emphasis on a disproportionately high rate of West Indian self-employment.

Unfortunately, West Indian businesses were almost never studied for themselves, but as a means of demonstrating the dismal rate of American-born blacks in business. The main objective of most of the scholars writing about the West Indian experience in America was to show how a West Indian premigration culture (which American-born blacks lacked) prepared these black foreigners for economic success in America. The immigrants' work ethic, acute sense of financial management, their clannishness as displayed by their familial and associational life, their proficiency in English, and their superior British education have all been advanced as traits that combined with the American context of economic opportunity to propel them toward a high rate of self-employ-ment. Although most of the analyses were impressionistic and almost all the examples drawn from New York, the stereotype of the successful West Indian entrepreneur in America was entrenched. As early as the 1920s, the term "Jewmaicans" had become a common label for this group, pointing to their propensity for thriftiness and self-employment.

Recently this stereotype has come under more careful scrutiny, revealing that West Indian success in business has been exaggerated.[2] While the revisionist studies have contributed to a fuller and more objective understanding of West Indian participation in business, the preoccupation with West Indians in New York still poses a setback. This essay seeks to move away from the traditional arena to study West Indians in Boston. It is not a discussion of West Indians vis-à-vis native African Americans, nor is it an exploration of how a black immigrant group surmounted racism or succumbed to it. The intent is to demonstrate how migration goals, cultural traditions, and structural opportunity all combined to determine the evolution of a systematic economic trajectory distinctive to the West Indian community in Boston.

West Indians, like most other immigrants, emigrated with the conviction that their move was temporary. Nevertheless, they came to Boston with well-formulated ideas about what the migration venture entailed and what it meant to succeed. Escaping severely impoverished economies, West Indian settlers came with a conscious plan to achieve the middle-class life that had eluded them in their homeland. The anecdotal data clearly demonstrate that for most of the immigrants the move to Boston was prompted by the search for economic stability, the fundamental ingredient most believed would give them access to middle-class status. Middle-class, as construed by these migrants, conformed to a West Indian variant, motivating them to pursue the same objectives that had determined middle-class standing in their native islands: a stable, well-paying job, a respectable profession such as law or medicine, a good education for their children, and, finally, that paramount indicator of middle-class status—home ownership.

The prerequisite for executing this master plan has been economic stability, the rationale being that with a stable job and enough earnings, one could educate one's children, send remittances home, own a home in Boston and possibly in the homeland as well, thus fulfilling the goals of migration. Little wonder, then, that the primary concern for the new-comers has been how to generate income that would ensure this kind of economic stability. Also clear to the newcomers, although often not initially, was the realization that they must attempt to generate income and achieve economic stability within a preexisting context over which they would have little control. Thus, they migrate with a definitive purpose, armed with a set of premigration values and experiences, but they must contend with the limitations of this new context.

It is the interplay of West Indian immigrant goals and characteristics within the social structure of Greater Boston that frames this study. The findings highlight the characteristic pragmatism of this group of black foreigners who, utilizing their premigration culture, capitalized on the nature of the city's economy to carve out their particular economic path. The following discussion unravels the immigrant economic trajectory by first describing West Indian patterns of self-employment, once thought to be the overriding determinant of this population's economic success in America. In what kind of businesses are Boston's West Indians involved? How do they set them up? What are their financial and social resources? Who are their employees and clientele? What kind of obstacles do they encounter? How much economic stability does self-employment provide for West Indians? The analysis generated by these questions will show that although West Indian immigrants are clearly among the ethnic groups in Boston that have increased their entrepreneurial activities in the last two decades, overall they have found their economic niche not in self-employment, but as wage earners in Boston's service-based economy.[3]

Boston's West Indian Community: An Overview

West Indians were among the first foreign-born blacks to migrate to Boston, their arrival dating as far back as the second half of the nineteenth century. However, the first major influx came with the outbreak of World War I, when immigration from Europe was drastically curtailed and West Indians, along with other peoples of the Western Hemisphere, were encouraged to relocate to the United States as replacement workers. This period also coincided with the introduction of the steamship passenger lines of the United Fruit Company to several ports in the Caribbean, thus facilitating travel from West Indian islands to harbors on the eastern seaboard of the United States. Although the overwhelming majority of these immigrants settled in New York City, Boston was also a major destination. This first wave was dominated by arrivals from three islands—Jamaica, Barbados, and Montserrat—and ended in the early 1950s, when restrictive U.S. immigration laws virtually put a stop to immigration from that region.

Throughout this initial flow the West Indian community in Boston was very small, their numbers never exceeding 5,000 (U.S. Department of Commerce 1913, 1922, 1932, 1943, 1952). Although they lived within a general black Boston community, they succeeded in creating a subculture that was underscored by their church participation, membership in voluntary associations, and publication of the *Boston Chronicle* newspaper.

The bulk of West Indians currently living in Boston arrived in the second wave, which effectively began in 1967 and continues strong to the present. This influx brought a phenomenal increase in the number of West Indians settling in Boston and other cities of the Northeast. The catalyst for this development was the Hart-Celler Immigration Act of 1965.[4] Three of its provisions in particular would ensure the dramatic rise in West Indian migration to the United States. First, the elimination of national quotas lifted the major obstacle to West Indian immigration, a hurdle that had been put into place with the passing of the McCarran-Walter Act of 1952, the policy that effectively stemmed the tide of the earlier wave of West Indian settlement. With the passing of the 1965 reforms the newly independent West Indian nations no longer had to scramble for the miserly one hundred slots for British colonies allowed under the 1952 law. Second, the family reunification provision of Hart-Celler allowed the immigrants to use established kinship networks to legally bring family members to this country. Finally, the occupational preference provision allowed West Indians, skilled and semiskilled, to migrate under the employer sponsorship program. In addition to accounting for the increase in the size of Boston's West Indian population, this latter provision has also shaped the contours of West Indian employment; a large proportion of those who have entered Boston's service wage economy got their start through the employer sponsorship program.

West Indians, who by 1960 were seeing the doors to the United Kingdom close on them, averted a demographic and economic catastrophe by taking advantage of a more generous U.S. immigration policy. Thus, according to INS and U.S. census records, only a decade after the 1965 reforms were implemented, West Indian immigration had exceeded that of the previous seventy years. By 1980, more than fifty thousand people from the English-speaking West Indies were entering the United States legally every year. As with the previous immigration wave, New York City continues to receive the overwhelming majority.

Although Boston received a sizable portion of the post-1965 arrivals, the official statistics do not adequately reflect this trend because most of the immigrants gave New York, their first U.S. port of disembarkation, as their destination. Community data clearly indicate that many West Indians now living in Boston moved there from other cities of the East Coast such as Providence, Rhode Island; Hartford, Connecticut; Miami, Florida; and especially New York City. This pattern was particularly prevalent in the late 1970s and early 1980s, when West Indians and other immigrants flocked into Boston to avail themselves of the opportunities provided by the expanding Massachusetts economy.

Official 1990 census figures are much lower, but an informal survey conducted in the late 1980s by one of the West Indian associations estimated that the total population of naturalized citizens, resident aliens, temporary workers, and undocumented immigrants numbered around forty thousand at least. In 1990 a Barbadian association, announcing plans for the celebration of the twenty-third anniversary of Barbados's independence, declared that the organizers "estimate that there were about fifty thousand transplanted Barbadians in the area." This disparity in figures demonstrates the frustration involved in trying to arrive at a precise picture of the size of Boston's West Indian population. However, from a synthesis of all the major sources—official figures and informal neighborhood or community data—it seems safe to project that the present size of the West Indian population of Boston is somewhere between fifty thousand and seventy thousand.

Although Jamaicans still constitute the largest contingent, the post-1965 West Indian population is far more diverse than the earlier wave. The community now consists of sizable numbers of such islanders as Trinidadians, Vincentians, and Antiguans (especially Trinidadians) who were virtually absent in the first wave. Furthermore, although the post-1965 immigration contained more educated and professional middle-class West Indians than the first wave, newcomers of working-class background still predominated.

West Indians in Boston have never forged a visible, physical ethnic enclave. The reasons are their relative small numbers and their tendency to dissipate, as it were, into the general black population of the city, with whom they share a common language—English. When the first wave of

West Indians came, they settled mostly in the South End and Lower Roxbury neighborhoods, among the black population, which during that time consisted mostly of migrants from the South. By the beginning of the second wave, Boston's black population had extended from the South End and Roxbury into the Dorchester and Mattapan sections of the city. The majority of post-1965 West Indian immigrants, like their predecessors, have followed the residential patterns of Boston's blacks, settling in Dorchester and Mattapan, with the highest concentration in Mattapan.

The absence of a recognizable, physical ethnic enclave notwithstanding, West Indians, starting with those of the first wave, have forged a viable West Indian subculture within the general black community of Greater Boston. The most visible indicator of this subculture is undoubtedly the annual Caribbean carnival. This event was inaugurated in 1974, according to the organizers, to affirm the increasing presence of West Indians in the Boston area. Since that time, on the last Saturday in August, a parade of West Indians in flamboyant carnival costumes dancing to calypso music travels along Blue Hill Avenue, the main thoroughfare of the West Indian community, finally dispersing in neighboring Franklin Park. Although even a casual look reveals the dominance of English-speaking West Indians in this event, it has increasingly become a pan-African celebration of blackness. Now represented in the parade are non-English-speaking West Indians, like Haitians and Panamanians, Africans, and African Americans, especially local African American politicians.

Although carnival organizers succeeded in getting the Massachusetts state government to declare the last week of August Caribbean Week, the carnival is no St. Patrick's Day Parade, the celebration being largely confined to the black community. This event, designed to underscore the presence of a foreign black group, is largely shunned by the mainstream news media, and the majority of Bostonians remain oblivious to its existence.

Several other institutions help define the West Indian subculture. One such institution is the church. Since the early 1920s many West Indians have attended and obtained membership in Roman Catholic and Protestant churches in their neighborhoods, which are predominantly African American. Three churches, because of their predominantly English-speaking West Indian congregations, could rightly be described as West Indian churches—St. Cyprian's Episcopal Church in Roxbury, Greenwood Memorial Methodist Church in Dorchester, and the Church of the Holy Spirit Episcopal in Mattapan. Besides having pastors who are from the islands, these churches have associations that organize activities representative of West Indian immigrant culture. In the earlier wave, St. Cyprian's, which is the oldest of the three churches, reflected a British–West Indian culture by organizing tea parties at which lectures were delivered. Today, the West Indian churches, including St. Cyprian's, have shifted from tea parties to events with a more indigenous West Indian flavor. This is especially true of their bazaars, which, in many ways, are like minicarnivals.

Most of the secular organizations are formed along national-island affiliations. In 1950, there were only about five major island associations and six sports or cricket clubs. These mushroomed after 1967 along with the West Indian population; by 1985 there were no fewer than thirty-five island associations and twenty pan–West Indian recreational associations. A significant portion of the endeavors of these associations is devoted to organizing recreational activities, such as dances and other festive events celebrating independence, anniversaries of the various West Indian countries, cricket matches between the Boston teams and West Indian teams in other northeastern cities, trips to carnivals in other North American cities, especially New York and Toronto, and activities celebrating U.S. holidays like Thanksgiving and the Fourth of July. Although these festive events, many of which feature homeland entertainers like reggae and calypso artists, are mainly recreational, they may also be fundraising charity ventures. Funds garnered from such activities are used to help West Indians, but not so much those in Boston as those in the homeland.[5]

No analysis of West Indian community institutions would be complete without some discussion of the rotating credit association. Called *partner* by Jamaicans and Barbadians and *susu* by Trinidadians, the rotating credit association is believed to reflect one of the vestiges of the African heritage in West Indian culture.[6] Under this system, which has been described by some scholars as indigenous banking, a group of people, usually from diverse islands but of the same socioeconomic stratum, decided to contribute a fixed amount of money (a *hand*) each week. The members of the group need not know each other. Usually the banker, who is responsible for collecting the weekly hand from each member, is the only one who needs to know how to contact each member of this informal network. The banker also arranges a schedule to determine whose turn it is each week to draw the pool. The draw is rotated each week until all members get their turn. At the end, which is usually several weeks, depending on the number of participants, they start all over again with a bigger or smaller number of members.[7] Although West Indian men participate in this institution, without a doubt it is the women who control it, both as bankers and participants. Only a few partners have men as organizers and bankers. Moreover, many of the men who participate do so through their wives or girlfriends who contribute two hands—one for themselves and the other for their husband or boyfriend.

This kind of banking has helped many of the immigrants make a successful economic adjustment to their new circumstances. The most advantageous facet of the system is that it serves as an ethnic bank where the immigrants, members of an underprivileged racial minority, can get credit without all the red tape of the formal financial institutions. The rotating credit groups mainly serve as a transplanted economic mechanism for first-generation immigrants and not necessarily as a continuing badge of ethnic identity. Nevertheless, it still stands as one of the features confirming the existence of a distinctive West Indian culture.

The West Indian Business Community

In the 1920s and 1930s especially, when New York's West Indians were being lauded for their propensity to operate small businesses, the state of black entrepreneurship in Boston was bleak. The situation remained the same throughout much of the first half of the twentieth century. This is not to say no successful businesses were owned and operated by blacks. The two black weekly publications of the period, the *Boston Guardian* and the *Boston Chronicle*, frequently brought attention to thriving black ventures, especially in the South End, while lamenting the overall low incidence of black self-employment.

West Indians as an entity within the larger black population had an even poorer rate of entrepreneurial participation. In 1940, the *Boston Chronicle*, which was owned by West Indian immigrants, conducted a survey of black businesses. The results showed that of the thirty establishments surveyed, only two had West Indian proprietors. The overwhelming majority were owned by African American men and women who had moved to Boston from other regions of the country at about the same time as the West Indians, most coming from the southern states of

Virginia, North and South Carolina, and Georgia, as well as the midwestern cities of Chicago and Detroit.

By the late 1970s, the state of black business enterprise in Boston had greatly improved. The main impetus for this shift was a classic case of ethnic succession, a process whereby the departure of one ethnic group from a neighborhood paves the way for the succeeding ethnic group to occupy the business void left by the departing population. In the 1960s and 1970s, there was a mass exodus of Jews from Roxbury, Dorchester, and Mattapan to suburbs like Milton and Randolph. Their departure left a commercial void in the neighborhood, especially along Blue Hill Avenue. Minority businesses—Hispanic, Asian (especially Korean), and black, including West Indian—were established to cater to the growing new consumer base, made up mostly of blacks, including West Indians, who were beginning to move into the houses of the departing Jewish residents. Old signs still hanging with the more imposing new ones serve as testimony to this ethnic succession.[8]

The emergence of greater numbers of West Indian businesses in the late 1970s and 1980s was, in large measure, a concomitant of the surge in the region's West Indian population resulting from both the expansive immigration policies and the draw of a favorable economic climate in Massachusetts. These enterprises are diverse, although most can be categorized as service businesses that target coethnics and the black population in general. Among them are food operations, including restaurant, bakery, and catering services; barber and beauty salons; moving companies; mechanic and panel beating shops; renovation contracting—carpentry, painting, electric wiring, and masonry; entertainment promotion; and small-scale retailing, especially in tropical foods, grocery, liquor, and convenience stores.

The food business is the most thriving. Restaurants and bakeries that deal in a variety of Caribbean dishes such as goat curry, rice and beans, jerk chicken, roti, beef patties, bread pudding, and other West Indian pastries are well patronized, not only by coethnics who yearn for familiar foods, but also by Americans, especially young African Americans. More than two-thirds of the businesses surveyed are sole proprietorships; a few are owned by two to four partners. Most such partnerships are with spouses or other close family members. The enterprises are managed by the owners themselves and family members. Generally, the number of employees, who are mostly fellow West Indians, is small, ranging from one to six depending on the type of venture. A few businesses, mostly barbershops and beauty salons, employ some African Americans, but none of those surveyed have white employees.

West Indian establishments share the same business district as other black enterprises. The only distinguishable West Indian shops, at first glance, are the restaurants, whose exteriors advertising their special dishes carry all the markings of a West Indian, Caribbean tropical flavor. A few of these West Indian businesses are located on Tremont Street in the South End, which is where West Indians of the first wave settled. The majority, however, are located in the Dorchester-Mattapan area, scattered along Blue Hill Avenue, from Franklin Park to Mattapan Square. The only thing akin to a cluster of West Indian shops can be found in the Codman Square area of Dorchester. Cambridge, which is home to about one-quarter of the West Indian population of Greater Boston, also has some West Indian enterprises, located mainly around the neighborhood of Central Square.

Who are the West Indian entrepreneurs? What financial and social resources do they have? And what are the factors that enhance or hamper their entrepreneurial endeavors? Although the majority of business owners are men, women are also represented, particularly in the restaurant and beauty enterprises. All the proprietors have at least a high school education or, more precisely, according to their homeland educational system, the Ordinary Levels Certificate. About 15 to 20 percent have tertiary education.

How much did their premigration economic experiences or activities prepare them, in fact prompt them, to set up small businesses? This question is especially important for those historians who have emphasized the significance of entrepreneurial heritage in opening and maintaining ethnic businesses in America. In much of the West Indies the business arena historically has been dominated by nonblack groups like East Indians, Chinese, Syrians, Lebanese, and Jews. This situation has prompted some observers to assert that Afro–West Indians are not enterprising and lack business acumen. Recent studies counter such views by showing that even in the preemancipation era blacks displayed remarkable entrepreneurial initiative.[9]

Black West Indians, however, like other colonized black populations, still became trapped within the value system of the colonial society. In that milieu, social mobility meant obtaining positions that the brown- and white-skinned members of the society occupied and living the lifestyle of those privileged groups. The most effective way to attain this goal was through higher education and respectable, stable, salaried employment within the government machinery. Thus, although it is a travesty to claim that West Indian blacks had no entrepreneurial heritage and no business proclivity, the enormous impact of the colonial value system on occupational patterns cannot be denied.[10]

The background of the majority of Boston's West Indian entrepreneurs accentuates this fact. Less than 5 percent of those interviewed had entrepreneurial experience before moving to Boston. They all acknowledged that they arrived in the United States guided by the value system of the society they had left behind. Therefore, they came hoping to acquire more education and advance into stable, salaried positions in the government or as successful professionals working for private companies. Most of them entered into small business not because of a pre-migration entrepreneurial tradition impelling them toward a familiar realm, but because of a pragmatic recognition of a broadening West Indian and black consumer base in need of service businesses. This adaptive modification of their goals led them to become what some scholars have referred to as culture entrepreneurs (Reeves and Ward 1984, 3).

Similarly, most of the owners reported that they did not come with the capital to start a business. Financial resources had to be sought in Boston. It is primarily for this reason that the West Indian immigrants had to be living in Boston for a length of time—an average of five years—before launching their businesses. Although a small percentage of the proprietors acknowledged help from banks and other formal lending sources, few attempts were made to go through such institutions for the initial start. A Trinidadian owner of a grocery store in the South End described his own experience in opening his business in the early 1980s: "When I started this business by selling some goat meat and a few other things, I did not go anywhere near a bank for money. I did not even think of trying. I mean it; the thought never even crossed my mind. I saved my money and got some help from my brother who is now like a partner in the business."

This reluctance to request loans from established lending institutions should not be seen as an aberration. West Indians have come from a society in which such formal organizations did very little to provide capital for business ventures. Like the Trinidadian cited above, most West Indian businessmen and women relied on their personal savings and assistance from family and friends. However, the evidence suggests that once their businesses got off the ground most went to banks and credit unions for loans to help maintain them.

The vitality of the support of the community has often been stressed in explaining social resources. For example, Scott Cummings expressed the view of many when he wrote: "The status of prosperous immigrant groups rests upon a collective and communitarian base" (1980, 17).[11] In the case of West Indians, this strong communitarian base, symbolized by kinship and associations, has continually been offered as the major factor in West Indian entrepreneurial success.[12] Findings from this study, however, indicate that community support for businesses was minimal, although as noted above, it was not unusual for family and kin to help in capital accumulation. Also, in some cases, family members worked in the businesses as formal or informal employees. Many of these family members, however, were new arrivals, in transition before absorption into the broader wage economy. Thus, even with familial support, the West Indian entrepreneurs in Boston displayed a strong individualism. As a Jamaican woman, a beauty salon owner, aptly described it: "My brother loaned me money, which I gave him back. My sisters and nieces sometimes work for me, but nothing permanent. You see, the main thing is that my business is my business. In spite of their help, my sweat is the most plentiful."

One major form of West Indian organization that is often advanced in the cultural argument as pivotal to successful entrepreneurship is the rotating credit association. Although some scholars, such as Ivan Light, have portrayed this institution as one of the main props of the West Indian business community, the extent of its role in providing financial resources for small businesses is debatable. Although many of the first generation, both male and female, are members of partners, most of them stated that they used their draws for nonbusiness ventures, such as passage money for relatives to emigrate, school fees, down payments for a home or an automobile, vacations to the homeland, and social events like weddings and christenings. A Trinidadian businessman who has been a *susu* banker since he came to Boston more than twenty years ago emphasized these functions of rotating credit in the economic and social adjustment of West Indian immigrants: "Since I came to this country I have organized a *susu* for which I am the banker. Every single year I look around and wonder how many houses, how many cars, how many plane tickets, and how many weddings the *susu* money has contributed to. Many fellas and ladies tell me what they plan to do when they come for their draws. So, a few weeks after, when I see them and see the results, I always shake my head with pleasure and say to myself, 'this is how to live in another country.' "

As for the more structured associations, for all their vibrancy, they pay virtually no attention to fostering the establishment and maintenance of coethnic businesses. These associations are active in organizing independence celebrations, the annual carnival, and other festivities. As a prominent Barbadian, who has been living in Boston for seventeen years, remarked: "We West Indians are very organization conscious people. We do very well in coming together to plan festive events—independence celebrations, dances, and bazaars. But after all the merriment we disband. We do not do much to help boost the economic status of West Indians as a community in the Boston society. The one good thing that we do, I must confess, is collect money, clothes, etc., to send for the needy people at home [in the West Indies]."

Some of the prominent businesspeople are also office holders in these associations and, thus, the principal organizers of recreational activities in Boston and of the homeland crusade. In fact, more than half the owners surveyed claimed they were active in one to three associations. Most of them did not seem to mind the separation of businesses from associations. One's economic endeavors might elicit envy and jealousy from fellow ethnics. Therefore, the less others knew, the better.

It is to their detriment that West Indian businesses have not yet evolved an organized interaction with their community institutions. Ample evidence testifies to the efficacy of such an affiliation. The Chinese, Koreans, and Vietnamese provide the best examples. In addition to a supportive kinship pattern, their associations, including rotating credit associations, serve as guilds that foster and promote business (Light 1972; Waldinger, Aldrich, and Ward 1989; Waldinger 1990). Between 1988 and 1990, a few West Indian business owners, aware of the benefits of such a dynamic relationship, made three unsuccessful attempts to establish their own trade associations.

The lack of associational support is just one of many factors that have undermined the growth of West Indian businesses. Another major drawback has been the market itself. West Indians in Boston have not been able to develop anything like a self-sufficient subethnic or enclave economy. Their relatively small numbers alone preclude that. Although a sizable portion of their customers are fellow West Indians, West Indian businesses rely heavily on African Americans and other blacks who live in the neighborhoods where their shops are located. As the owners confirmed, service businesses like restaurants, hairdressing establishments, mechanic's shops, and entertainment enterprises experience little difficulty in attracting and keeping this black clientele.

The biggest problem is with retail businesses. Other ethnics, especially Hispanics and Koreans, have capitalized on being in the same neighborhoods by dealing in products that are West Indian, and on a much larger scale than West Indian retail ventures. Korean produce stores on the South End–Chinatown boundary carry a variety of tropical produce such as green bananas, sweet potatoes, and yams. Korean fish markets in the South End, Dudley, and Dorchester neighborhoods are well stocked with porgie, codfish, and snapper, all West Indian favorites. On the shelves of Hispanic tropical food stores are such West Indian fare as ackee, sorrel, and goat meat, and in the cooked food sections, hot Jamaican beef patties. All these Hispanic and Asian enterprises are well patronized by the West Indian community, a trend that has caused the few West Indian retailers to complain that their businesses are not being frequented by coethnics as much as they would have liked. A Jamaican convenience store owner expressed the sentiments of many of his coethnics when he lamented: "We are not many, I agree, but the few numbers we have feel better going to other people to buy. Why? They say they do not trust us, that we cheat. The same thing they did in Jamaica—going to buy from the Chinese—is happening here. That is why the best thing to do is open a restaurant and cook your own food, which the American, Puerto Rican, or Korean cannot cook."

But without a doubt, none of the above obstacles has had as devastating an effect as racism and its attendant features of discrimination and segregation. Since the first wave, West Indians have consistently tried to uphold a foreign identity. But ultimately they find themselves existing within the structural parameters of the Boston African American community.[13] This alone has had some adverse effects on West Indian entrepreneurship. The majority of these businesses are situated in predominantly black neighborhoods, which are the most impoverished and crime-ridden sections of the city. Thus, many West Indian proprietors contend that they are compelled to deal not only with a financially weak clientele, but also with relatively more physical risks, a factor that has a discouraging effect on prospective clients who do not live in these neighborhoods.[14] Valid as this concern is, the argument becomes problematic when one considers the success rate of some of the other ethnic establishments that share the same locations as West Indian and other black enterprises. Koreans, especially, have carried on thriving businesses in black neighborhoods in Boston and other American cities.

Perhaps less problematic to decipher are the problems encountered in gaining access to loans. Initially the majority of West Indian businesses were started without help from lending institutions such as banks. Later, however, many turn to such sources for assistance in expanding the businesses or saving them. Many of those interviewed, about 75 percent of the total number, claimed they had experienced racism in securing loans from Boston banks. As with most groups that claim to be victims of racism and discrimination, West Indian entrepreneurs could not clearly convey the basis for their charges. Questions in the interviews were phrased and rephrased to help bring out substantial, tangible reasons to support claims of racism. But most of the time the answers seemed to make the same vague assertion—"I did not get the loan because I am a black person and the bankers, who are mostly whites, do not like blacks." But there could be other reasons: How viable did the banks consider the businesses the applicants were proposing to expand or save? How substantial was the collateral presented? Did the fact that some of them were resident aliens and not citizens create reservations in the mind of the loan officer who may have considered them a risk?

A significant break in empirical investigation, clearly confirming the claims of the interviewees, came in 1991 with the release of the results of a Federal Reserve study that unequivocally concluded that minorities, especially blacks, routinely faced serious discrimination when they applied for loans. Moreover, among all cities in the United States, Boston ranked an infamous number one for rejection of black loan applications for mortgages.[15]

All these drawbacks—lack of ethnic solidarity, disadvantageous business locations, stiff competition from other ethnic groups, and racism—have combined to stifle the growth of West Indian small business ventures. Although some of the enterprises, especially restaurant and food catering operations, are doing well, the general rate of success remains relatively modest. Most of the problems emanate from the opportunity structure, and this economic and occupational context in many ways has been eroding West Indian entrepreneurship.

West Indians and Boston's Service-Based Economy

The same opportunity structure that serves to constrain West Indian business initiatives has simultaneously been propitious for another sector of the immigrant community, namely, wage earners in the service economy. The Hart-Celler Act, under whose largess most of them came, facilitated their entry into the service economy. The overwhelming majority arrive prepared to prosper through it. About half of those West Indians entering after 1965 migrated under the employer sponsorship program. Most of them were sponsored by American families and agencies to come as household workers. Even those who did not arrive under the program were assisted by family and kin in obtaining domestic work. Very often they adjusted their "B" or tourist visas to worker visas once they had found families or agencies who would sponsor them. Domestic work was, however, usually just a springboard. After two or three years, most moved on to other areas of the service economy.

This relatively easy absorption into and movement within the service sector has been possible because of some advantages. The first is their knowledge of English, having come from countries whose official language is English. Even their lingua franca, patois, is a corrupt form of English. Language has been a most useful edge, as most of them had no experience in the service sector occupations that they eventually entered.[16]

Knowledge of English and an effective kinship network would not have been so advantageous had not the economic structure been favorable. By the time the second wave of West Indians started arriving in Boston, the city was successfully moving from trade and manufacturing to a service-based economy. The boom in the economy that followed made the shift complete. In 1982, of all the nation's thirty-four largest metropolitan areas, Boston was ranked third in services, after Washington, D.C., and New York City (Mitchell 1988, 10). Most of the jobs created by such a service-based economy, however, are low-paying positions with limited opportunity for career advancement.[17] In spite of this daunting reality, West Indians have availed themselves of the existence of plentiful employment, especially before 1989, to work overtime, often holding two jobs. Although they are fairly dispersed in the service industries, health care is where West Indians are most concentrated, as nurses, lab technicians, medical records clerks, nurses' aides, orderlies, and housekeepers.

Although laboring for wages in the service sector demanded extremely long hours if they wanted to make decent earnings, it advanced their economic stability. Most of these West Indian workers acknowledged both the sacrifices and rewards. A nursing assistant from Jamaica related a common experience: "I never worked like this before in my life—long hours and hard work. But the money is good. When the agency called me to go work, I hold the phone and want to say no, then I think about the paycheck. Then I think about my sister who wants to come; and my house in Montego Bay that I want to finish building. Then I quickly say: 'I will do it, give me the directions to the nursing home.' "

West Indian women, especially, have benefited from this context. They have more opportunities as nurses' aides in hospitals and nursing homes and as home health aides and homemakers. Between 1985 and 1987 in particular, the health care industry of Boston was very prosperous, especially in the area of elderly care. Nursing personnel agencies sprang up around the city, and many West Indian women worked for these agencies as nurses' aides and homemakers for the elderly, in addition to their full-time jobs in hospitals and nursing homes. In those years, eighty-hour work weeks were not uncommon. This earned the women as much as seven hundred dollars a week, an amount that most could never make as profit from a business in the most depressed section of the city.

The service sector afforded West Indian immigrants, especially the women, the economic stability that they craved. This in turn gave them the potential to achieve other objectives of migration, such as good, private schools for their children, home ownership, vacations to the homeland, and passage money for relatives at home to join them in Boston. Black political activists in Boston urge black residents to be more involved in business as a way of advancing the status of the group. However, individual West Indians are finding their goals fulfilled not in entrepreneurship but in the service sector.

An increasing number of West Indian women own their own business or are co-owners with their spouses or some other male relative, but the lure of economic stability through wage labor in the service sector reduces their participation in small business. About one-third of the proprietors, both male and female, routinely operate their ventures while working part-time in a service industry within the larger Boston economy.

Many of the positive group characteristics that are often emphasized in relation to West Indians' success in self-employment are amply reflected in their endeavors as wage earners in the broader service economy. The ethic of hard work and sacrifice is displayed in the long overtime hours. Also, unlike the case of business, much stronger ethnic solidarity is displayed in their wage-earning efforts. West Indian immigrants have made such significant inroads in the lower levels of certain service institutions that through family and kin networks they are able to facilitate the entry of new arrivals and ensure their retention.[18] Nursing homes and hospitals, especially, reflect this ethnic solidarity among West Indian employees. American employers and managers for their part have tacitly encouraged the clustering of particular ethnic workers to ensure employee competence and loyalty.

Boston, like most major cities in the United States, has witnessed a remarkable growth in immigrant or ethnic enterprise since the 1970s. West Indians are undoubtedly a part of that phenomenon, as businesses that dot certain major streets in the neighborhoods of Roxbury, Dorchester, and Mattapan exemplify, with their colorful exteriors of palm and coconut tree paintings and the bright colors of flags of West Indian nations. Also in clear view from the display windows are flyers, pamphlets, and posters advertising upcoming events in the West Indian and African American communities. Visible as this entrepreneurial side of Boston's West Indian community is, business owners are still a minute fraction of the total West Indian immigrant population. The vast majority channel their energies and social resources into the Boston service economy, which, in spite of its many flaws, provides an avenue for economic stability. According to the 1990 census, more than 82 percent of West Indian newcomers live above the poverty line. In the grand migration design, this element of economic stability is the most crucial. For it is the tool that enables these immigrants to achieve most of the goals that they set out to pursue in the United States.

Notes

1. The terms "West Indians" and "British West Indians" are used interchangeably in this study to refer to black immigrants from English-speaking Caribbean countries such as Jamaica, Barbados, Trinidad and Tobago, Montserrat, the Virgin Islands, and Guyana, which geographically is in South America but has a cultural West Indian identity. Some well-known West Indians who wrote about the West Indian propensity for business were Domingo (1925), first-generation Jamaican activist in New York; McKay (1940), first-generation Jamaican writer and activist; Reid (1939) second-generation West Indian; Johnson (1930), second-generation West Indian.

2. See, for example, Allen and Farley (1987); Model (1992); Kasinitz (1992), especially chap. 3.

3. Conclusions presented in this chapter are drawn largely from data collected

from in-depth, open-ended interviews with twenty-seven West Indian owners of small businesses, twenty nonbusiness West Indians, and eleven American employers or supervisors. These interviews were conducted between September 1990 and July 1991. English was the medium of communication, although some of the respondents kept switching from English to their native patois, broken or pidgin English. Participant observation was an important part of my data collection. I attended church services, where first contact with most of my respondents was made. Most of the introductions were done by ministers who, as mediators, provided the legitimacy that I needed for my respondents to trust me, a non–West Indian, although I am also a foreign–born black. Cultural events like the West Indian annual carnival held in August and independence celebrations, especially the former, gave me significant insights into the dynamics of the community. I also visited association clubs and spoke with their office holders. The social and family gatherings to which I was invited, such as weddings, christenings, and Thanksgiving dinners, provided additional opportunities for understanding a people's culture.

4. For details on the unanticipated consequences of the Hart-Celler Immigration Act, see Reimers (1983).

5. Most of the funds acquired by West Indian associations are used to assist victims of natural disasters in the islands and for educational development projects, such as establishing scholarships and purchasing and donating books and other school supplies.

6. Most West African societies have an identical system. The Yorubas of Nigeria call it *Esusu*, a term that is very close to the Trinidadian *susu.*

7. For more on this West Indian banking system as practiced in the homeland and by immigrants to the United States, see Katzin (1959); Bonnett (1981).

8. A good analysis of this ecological or demographic explanation for changes in ethnic businesses is Aldrich and Reiss (1976); for more on the departure of Jews from Roxbury, Dorchester, and Mattapan, see Ginsberg (1975), and Levine and Harmon (1992); one of the most graphic examples of this transition is a West Indian restaurant that has the Caribbean Cuisine and Jewish Kosher signs hanging prominently side by side on the storefront.

9. For a good example of how racial stratification in the West Indies is reflected in the business arena, see Stone (1991); for a discussion of nonblack groups and business in the West Indies, which includes such themes as their rate of participation, theories explaining why they do well in business, and how the black majority react to their economic positions, see Levy (1986); Nicholls (1986); Camejo (1971); Fortune (1984); for more on Afro–West Indians and business, especially in the era before emancipation, see Simmonds (1987); Mintz (1955).

10. For more on the British colonial influence see Nunes (1973); Hall (1968).

11. The significance of social resources is also discussed in Waldinger (1989, 56–58).

12. See, for example, the argument in Reid (1939); Haynes (1912); Light (1972); Sowell (1975).

13. The issue of West Indians, race, and identity is dealt with in depth in Johnson (1992); see especially chap. 4.

14. This concern has some validity. The *Boston Globe* ran an article showing the detrimental effects of a depressed and unsafe neighborhood on business. Although the piece did not focus on minority businesses, the discussion showed how large American retail chains, such as Star Market, Stop and Shop, Purity Supreme, and

CVS, either completely shun minority areas like Roxbury, Dorchester, and Mattapan or go into them reluctantly ("Why Retailers Shun Boston's Minority Neighborhoods," *Boston Sunday Globe,* 25 August 1991).

15. The study found that blacks in Boston with incomes of more than forty-five thousand dollars a year were turned down more often than whites with incomes of less than thirty-thousand dollars (*Boston Globe,* 22 October 1991).

16. Although West Indian women have been known for their efficiency in domestic service, most of those who came after 1965 had no prior experience. For many, it was an occupational demotion considering that they had been clerks, teachers, seamstresses, and so on. Even in the health care sector where most West Indians eventually worked as nurses aides and orderlies, they had little experience. Although a large number of nurses emigrated from Jamaica and Barbados in the 1970s, the majority went to New York City. Only a very small number, less than 5 percent of West Indian nurses in Boston, received their nursing training in the West Indies.

17. This phenomenon as it relates to Boston is thoughtfully tackled by Philip Bennet, "Just a Paycheck, Not an Opportunity," *Boston Globe Magazine,* 15 December 1985.

18. In the course of my research, I discovered that some Jamaican women who work as nursing assistants have organized informal training programs to acquaint new arrivals with the nursing home environment and to prepare them for interviews so that they can claim to have had some experience in nursing assistantship.

References

Aldrich, Howard, John Cater, Trevor Jones, David McEvoy, and Paul Velleman. 1985. "Ethnic Residential Concentration and the Protected Market Hypothesis." *Social Forces* 63: 996–1009.

Aldrich, Howard and Albert Reiss. 1976. "Continuities in the Study of Ecological Succession: Changes in the Race Composition of Neighborhoods and Their Businesses." *American Journal of Sociology* 81: 846–66.

Allen, Walter, and Reynolds Farley. 1987. *The Color Line and the Quality of Life: The Problem of the Twentieth Century.* New York: Russell Sage Foundation.

Bolles, Lynn A. 1981. "Goin' Abroad: Working-Class Jamaican Women and Migration." In *Female Immigrants to the United States: Caribbean, Latin American, and African Experiences,* edited by Delores M. Mortimer and Roy Simon Bryce-Laporte. Washington, D.C.: Smithsonian Institution.

Bonnett, Aubrey. 1981. *Institutional Adaptation of West Indian Immigrants to America: An Analysis of Rotating Credit Associations.* Washington, D.C.: University Press of America.

Butler, John Sibley. 1991. *Entrepreneurship and Self-Help among Black Americans: A Reconsideration of Race and Economics.* Albany: State University of New York Press.

Camejo, Acton. 1971. "Racial Discrimination and Employment in Trinidad and Tobago: A Study of the Business Elite and the Social Structure." *Social and Economic Studies* 20.

Cobas, Jose A. 1986. "Paths to Self-Employment among Immigrants: An Analysis of Four Interpretations." *Sociological Perspectives* 29: 101–20.

• The Case of British West Indians in Boston •

Cummings, Scott. 1980. *Self-Help in Urban America: Patterns of Minority Business Enterprise.* London: Kennikat Press.

Domingo, Wilfred A. 1925. "The Tropics in New York." *Survey Graphic* 6: 648–51.

Fortune, Stephen Alexander. 1984. *Merchants and Jews: The Struggle for British West Indian Commerce, 1650–1750.* Gainesville: University Press of Florida.

Ginsberg, Yona. 1975. *Jews in a Changing Neighborhood: The Study of Mattapan.* London: Free Press.

Hall, Douglas. 1968. "The Colonial Legacy in Jamaica." *New World Quarterly* 4: 7–23.

Haynes, Edmund. 1912. *The Negro at Work in New York City.* New York: Arno Press.

Johnson, James Weldon. 1930. *Black Manhattan.* New York: Knopf.

Johnson, Violet M. 1992. "The Migration Experience: Social and Economic Adjustment of British West Indian Immigrants in Boston." Ph.D. diss. Boston College.

Kasinitz, Philip. 1992. *Caribbean New York: Black Immigrants and the Politics of Race.* Ithaca: Cornell University Press.

Katzin, M. F. 1959. "Partners: An Informal Savings Institution in Jamaica." *Social and Economic Studies* 7: 436–40.

Levine, Hillel and Lawrence Harmon. 1992. *The Death of an American Jewish Community: A Tragedy of Good Intentions.* New York: Free Press.

Levy, Jacqueline. 1986. "The Economic Role of the Chinese in Jamaica: The Grocery Retail Trade." *The Jamaica Historical Review* 15: 31–50.

Light, Ivan. 1972. *Ethnic Enterprise in America.* Berkeley: University of California Press.

McKay, Claude. 1940. *Harlem: A Negro Metropolis.* New York: E. P. Dutton.

Mintz, Sidney. 1955. "The Jamaican Internal Marketing System." *Social and Economic Studies.*

Mitchell, Rudy. 1988. *Boston: A Socio-Economic and Religious Profile.* Boston: Emmanuel Gospel Center, Research Department.

Model, Suzanne. 1991. "Caribbean Immigrants: A Black Success Story?" *International Migration Review* 14: 248–76.

Mortimer, Delores M. 1981. "Race, Ethnicity, and Sex in the Recent Immigration." In *Female Immigrants to the United States: Caribbean, Latin American, and African Experiences,* edited by Delores M. Mortimer and Roy Simon Bryce-Laporte. Washington, D.C.: Smithsonian Institution.

Nicholls, David. 1986. "The Syrians of Jamaica." *Jamaica Historical Review* 15.

Nunes, Fred. 1973. "Social Structure, Values, and Business Policy in the Caribbean." *Caribbean Quarterly* 19: 62–75.

Portes, Alejandro and Leif Jensen. 1987. "What's an Ethnic Enclave? The Case for Conceptual Clarity: A Comment." *American Sociological Review* 52: 768–70.

Reeves, Frank and Robin Ward. 1984. "West Indian Business in Britain." In *Ethnic Communities in Business: Strategies for Economic Survival.* Cambridge: Cambridge University Press.

Reid, Ira De A. 1939. *The Negro Immigrant: His Background, Characteristics, and Social Adjustment, 1899–1937.* New York: AMS Press.

Reimers, David M. 1983. "An Unintended Reform: The 1965 Immigration Act and Third World Immigration to the United States." *Journal of American Ethnic History* (fall): 9–28.

Simmonds, Lorna. 1987. "Slave Higglering in Jamaica, 1780–1834." *Jamaica Journal* 20.

Sowell, Thomas. 1975. *Race and Economics*. New York: David McKay.

Stone, Carl. 1991. "Race and Economic Power in Jamaica." In *Garvey, His Work and Impact,* edited by Rupert Lewis and Patrick Bryon. Trenton, N.J.: Africa World Press.

U.S. Department of Commerce, Bureau of the Census, 1913. *Thirteenth Census of the United States: 1910*. Washington, D.C.: Government Printing Office.

——. 1922. *Fourteenth Census of the United States: 1920*. Washington, D.C.: Government Printing Office.

——. 1932. *Fifteenth Census of the United States: 1930*. Washington, D.C.: Government Printing Office.

——. 1943. *Sixteenth Census of the United States: 1940*. Washington, D.C.: Government Printing Office.

——. 1952. *A Report of the Seventeenth Decennial Census of the United States: 1950*. Washington, D.C.: Government Printing Office.

U.S. Department of Justice. 1960–88. *Statistical Year Book of the Immigration and Naturalization Service*. Washington, D.C.: U.S. Government Printing Office.

Waldinger, Roger. 1989. "Structural Opportunity or Ethnic Advantage? Immigrant Business Development in New York." *International Migration Review* 23.

Waldinger, Roger, Howard Aldrich, and Robin Ward. 1990. *Immigrant Entrepreneurs: Immigrant Business in Europe and the United States*. Newbury Park, Calif.: Sage.

Ward, Robin and Howard Aldrich. 1985. "Ethnic Business and Occupational Mobility in Advanced Societies." *Sociology* 19: 586–97.

Photo Essay

Boston's Immigrants in Business

Photographs by Steven J. Gold

Text by Marilyn Halter

Although their numbers, residential concentration, and business endeavors do not constitute a fully developed enclave, certain neighborhoods in the Greater Boston area do support aggregate Khmer enterprises. These coethnic businesses are part of a cluster that lines several adjoining streets in Revere.

This bustling Khmer grocery store is packed with people on a typical Sunday morning. Because the customers work such long hours during the rest of the week, Sunday mornings have become the preferred time to complete the household shopping.

Many ethnic enterprises offer a variety of services or products within a single, small establishment. In this Khmer photo store the owner provides professional photographic services, sells and develops film, and is also a videographer. Part of his business includes a courier service for the transfer of money, small goods, and letters to compatriots in Cambodia. Videotapes are made as proof that the items have been properly received. The proprietor is shown playing such a video for a customer. The tapes also carry messages and news, facilitating communication between the refugees and those at home.

While we were in the photo shop, a shipment of clothing arrived from Cambodia. Women and children gather in the studio area to try on and select garments.

In most immigrant food businesses, American influences are evident. At this Khmer restaurant, crates of the traditional soya bean beverage are stacked next to the universal Coke cans and other typical American soft drinks.

The proprietor sitting in the window of this salon uses creams derived from recipes passed on to her from her own parents, who were skin care specialists in their native city of Odessa. She runs the operation while her husband helps her out by keeping the books, a reversal of the traditional division of labor within a family business. Like many Soviet Jewish enterprises, this one caters to a non-coethnic clientele. The shop is located in one of the most upscale neighborhoods of Greater Boston.

In this popular Russian Jewish deli and grocery store, the owner stands in front of her well-stocked shelves of imported jams, jellies, and dried fruits. The sign above these food items means *books*, signaling that Russian reading matter is for sale in the space behind the groceries.

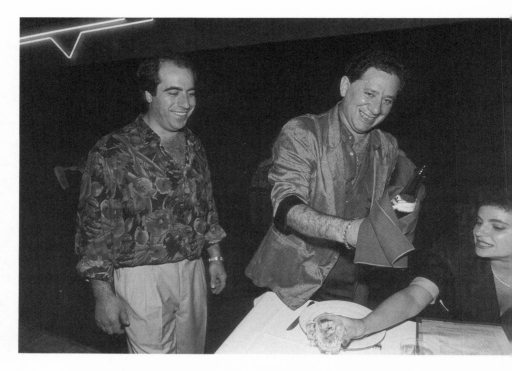

Russian restaurants such as this one also serve as community social centers for the celebration of birthdays, Bar and Bas Mitzvahs, weddings, and the like. A huge hall, live music, and a large dance floor make this a favorite spot for such gatherings.

On the walls of this long-established West Indian barbershop are displayed a variety of ethnic and racial images. A picture of Martin Luther King Jr. and Malcolm X hangs atop a banner from Trinidad and Tobago. The owner's love of sports is represented in the background by a newspaper photo of Joe Louis and a poster of the Boston Celtics. Customers include both West Indians and African Americans.

This West Indian bakery, one of the community's largest businesses, is frequented primarily by coethnics. It offers a wide array of Caribbean breads and pastries, and tropical drinks. Lunch and dinner items may be eaten on the premises or prepared for take-out.

The Best in Town West Indian Restaurant, like many of this ethnic population's enterprises, is located in an area of the city that is not the best, making it difficult to attract a wider clientele and keep the business thriving.

The proprietor of Andrea's Fashions stocks Spanish-language and music cassettes, as well as clothing for all ages.

This tiny bodega crammed with goods is located on a street where a number of Latino businesses are clustered, including Andrea's Fashions, another clothing store, two restaurants, a video store, and a gift shop.

Three generations of Greek immigrants are depicted in the two stores owned by this family. Grandmother and granddaughter stand in front of the shelves of knick-knacks in the gift shop. The little girl's father at left operates the European-style furniture store directly across the street.

The proprietor of one of the many pizza parlors owned by Greek immigrants in Boston stands proudly with his daughter who works in the restaurant part-time in the classic family business.

Chapter 5

Greek-American Economic Culture: The Intensification of Economic Life and a Parallel Process of Puritanization

Caesar Mavratsas

Greek immigrants throughout the United States have exhibited a consistent overrepresentation in ethnic entrepreneurialism and constitute one of the paradigmatic cases of middleman adjustment to American society (Fratoe and Meeks 1985, i; Moskos 1989, 22). This study draws on qualitative research on first-generation Greek-American entrepreneurs in the Greater Boston area and analyzes some of the basic features of Greek-American immigrant economic culture.[1] The aim of the chapter is twofold: first, to elucidate how the "transplanted cultural endowment" of Greek immigrants influences their economic life in America and the common Greek-American pattern of disproportionate entrepreneurialism (Light 1984, 199); second, to explain some of the differences that develop between the economic culture of Greek-America and that of mainland Greece.

What is unique about any particular ethnic group can be best understood if the experience of other groups, both similar and dissimilar, is taken into consideration. I examine Greek-American immigrant economic culture primarily in comparison to the economic culture of mainland Greece, but also to the economic culture of other immigrant groups in America. The analytical aim of this series of comparisons is to isolate the unique combination of factors that account for the formation of the distinct sociological entity, the Greek-American economic culture. The dominant feature of this entity is a disproportionate propensity for ethnic entrepreneurialism, a phenomenon that is, and always has been, a fundamental element of Greek-American life. The small entrepreneur has been the most important social type in terms of the sociohistorical development of Greek-American institutions and culture (Burghess 1913; Lovell-Troy 1980, 1981; Malafouris 1948; Moskos 1982, 1989; Papaioannou 1985; Saloutos 1964; Scourby 1984; Vlachos 1968; Zotos 1976). Greek-America is by no means a homogeneous entity, and it includes occupational groups other than its ethnic entrepreneurs. But the lifestyle and values of the latter have permanently and significantly stamped what may be called the basic Greek-American culture and identity.

The present analysis of the formation of Greek-American economic culture is based on in-depth interviews with Greek-Americans in the Greater Boston area—primarily, but not exclusively, first-generation small entrepreneurs. I have focused attention on those issues that the interviewees themselves considered important with regard to Greek-American entrepreneurialism and its role in the development of ethnic life and identity. The usual tendency in the study of ethnic entrepreneurialism and, more generally, of ethnicity has been to examine ethnic-immigrant groups in America in almost total abstraction from their mainland societies and culture; thus, the economic culture of immigrant groups in America is rarely compared to the economic culture of their homelands. The interviews I conducted dictated that a comparison between Greek-America and mainland Greece acquire a major portion of the analytical space with which the study is concerned. First-generation Greek-Americans think of and understand themselves primarily in contrast and comparison to mainland Greeks. Although they initially think of themselves merely as Greek, they eventually develop an indigenous and unavoidably hybrid identity as Greek-Americans. A significant part of this identity consists of explicit contrasts between Greek-Americans (us) and mainland Greeks (them).[2] The Greek-American propensity for ethnic entrepreneurialism, I suggest, is a result of the cultural baggage that Greek immigrants bring with them and the various transformations that it undergoes in American society.

Cultural Endowment and Ethnic Entrepreneurialism

The economic ethos that Greek immigrants bring with them consists of a peculiar type of individualistic nuclear familism that promotes the mobility and differentiation of its members, and strong urban and commercial orientations (Campbell 1974; Friedl 1964; Loizos 1975; McNeil 1978; Monos 1976; Sanders 1962; Tavouchis 1972). The influence of this cultural baggage is evident in the decision to become self-employed and the manner in which a business is started, the operation of such businesses, and their potential for success or failure. The economic ethos of the Greek immigrant promotes—or, to use Weberian terminology, places psychological premiums on—types of behavior and, more generally, a way of life that make ethnic entrepreneurialism the culturally preferred occupational option of Greek immigrants.

The Decision to Become Self-Employed

Greek peasants who emigrated to the United States did not have any skills that could be put to immediate use in their new environment. Thus, their immediate occupational options included only low-paying menial jobs. In this respect, they were not much different from immigrants from other countries. Greek immigrants, however, were more likely than most other immigrants with seemingly similar premigration experiences to quickly stop working for someone else and start their own businesses. The desire to become self-employed—a desire that is usually manifest from the first days a Greek immigrant sets foot in America—is clearly a function of the Greek's traditional value of independence. The Greek peasant participates in an economy in which the family is the preferred work unit. Being an *ipallilos* (employee; literally, "one who is under another") is thought to seriously hamper one's *philotimo* (love and pursuit of honor), which is the raison d'être of the Greek, and, by extension, that of his family (Campbell 1974; Loizos 1975; Peristiany 1974). The strong valuation of self-employment is one of the dominant aspects of the Greek-American ethos, and Greeks who arrived in America found themselves in an environment in which "wherever one turned, the admonition was to work hard, save, invest, succeed, become independent, and 'be your own boss' " (Saloutos 1964, 258).

A strong desire to become self-employed, and the ability to do so, however, are two different things. Greek immigrants have the former. They also have what may be loosely called the cultural capital with which to engage in commercially entrepreneurial activities. In Greek agriculture, goods are produced primarily to be sold in a market, and profitability depends greatly on business decisions that peasants often have to make in situ (McNeil 1978). Given Greek immigrants' familiarity with commercial endeavors and possession of market skills, the idea of starting one's own business is part of their cultural repertoire. Greeks who emigrate to America come from an environment in which *epichirimatikotita* (entrepreneurialism) is the sine qua non of economic success. They find themselves in a milieu in which this orientation is similarly rewarded.

Small business constitutes the culturally preferred occupational option of Greek immigrants. It affords them a sense of personal self-determination and is a type of work that has a strong affinity with the intense nuclear familism of the Greeks. Owning and operating a small business allows the immigrant to bring his entire family into the workplace, and, thus, to emulate the work situation with which he is familiar and in which the nuclear family is not only the structurally primary economic unit but also the culturally preferred one. Although the basic pattern of Greek emigration to America centered around initial waves of young single men, the appeal of occupations with the potential of incorporating the entire nuclear family has always been great. In Greek-America, having a small business and having a family come to be seen as essentially intertwined (especially after the idea of permanent residence in America crystallizes in the mind of the Greek immigrant).

The desire of Greek immigrants to become self-employed is even stronger because they come to America with the intention of "making it" financially and returning to Greece within a few years. Greek society has a relatively fluid class structure, and an important concomitant of this factor on the level of consciousness is a high achievement motivation (Loizos 1975; McNeil 1978; Rosen 1959). The latter becomes more intensified among Greek immigrants because the act of emigration was undertaken for economic motives and, thus, places them in a situation in which they face what researchers have called a "pressure" to succeed (Monos 1976). The Greek immigrant to America, thus, sees economic achievement as an imperative and realizes that owning his own business is the best and fastest way to achieve this goal. The people he envies or admires in the Greek-American community are self-made businessmen; it is these people who serve as his role models.

The relative ease and rapidity with which former peasants turn themselves into entrepreneurs may initially seem strange. After all, these are predominantly people with little formal education, few financial assets, limited knowledge of English, and little familiarity with the workings of American society. One might not expect them to turn immediately toward entrepreneurial endeavors. That Greek-Americans have done so, I propose, is clearly an indication of the adaptability of the Greek mind. This adaptability can be seen as a concomitant of the commercialism and urban orientation characteristic of Greek society. It is one of the factors that explains the Greek immigrant's determination to learn a new type of work and venture into an occupational area that contains more risks than most others.

Greek-American entrepreneurs usually start their careers in ethnic entrepreneurialism by working in coethnic enterprises of the type to which they plan to commit themselves. During this apprentice period they begin to learn the more technical and logistical aspects of the business. The entire Greek community, however, consists of ethnic networks that serve as a source of information and assistance regarding the initiation of small business establishments. The Greek immigrant is continuously exposed to talk about business opportunities, and it would not be an exaggeration to say that he begins his entrepreneurial career from the moment he arrives in America and converses with fellow immigrants.

Greek-American entrepreneurs usually capitalize their first business through the savings amassed after their arrival in America. Their first few years in their adopted country are characterized by a frugal way of life, and they are always willing and proud to reminisce about *ta prota chronia stin Ameriki* (the first years in America), and the hardships they lived through. Typically, immigrants save most of what they earn by not incurring any personal expenses. The immigrant initially lives with relatives or shares an apartment with coethnics, thus saving on rent. By spending most of their time at the workplace, immigrants can keep expenses almost at subsistence level. Greek immigrants perceive this ascetic life-style in an almost heroic mode. They see it as yet another manifestation of the agonistic spirit and toughness necessary for succeeding in life. They are willing to sacrifice for the years to come, which connotes a strong future orientation that may be linked to the proto-modern character of Greek culture.

The Operation of Greek-American Enterprises

Given the intense nuclear familism of Greek immigrants and the role this plays in their decision to become self-employed, it is only natural that most Greek-American small enterprises are owned and operated by the entrepreneurs and their families, without much reliance on outside labor. With a continuous effort to minimize the latter, Greek-American entrepreneurs exhibit a serious reluctance to trust or delegate authority to strangers (*xenoi*), that is, people outside the immediate nuclear family. It is generally believed that one cannot really rely upon unrelated persons and that to do so could be financially harmful.

Greek-American entrepreneurs and their families perform most of the necessary tasks in the business. Thus, it is not surprising that their workdays tend to be long and tiring. They consider their work ethic a necessary ingredient of the agonistic orientation toward life. Although hard work is not an anthropological constant, it often appears to be so for Greek immigrant entrepreneurs whose entire life seems to be centered around their business.

The Greek-American family business is not an egalitarian institution. The wife of the entrepreneur, who may often work harder in the business than her husband, does not usually have a say in major decisions and financial dealings concerning the family establishment. The Greek ethnic entrepreneur, a predominantly male element, tries to have as much personal control over the business as possible, and in doing so he often clashes with other family members—the wife, but more often the son, who expects eventually to take over the business—who may have their own opinions on how to perform tasks in the family enterprise.

Working for the family business is usually not rewarded with regular pay and benefits. Given the familial character of the Greek-American business, the latter would be unthinkable. Even to say that family members are employed in the business is rather misleading. The wife and children of the Greek ethnic entrepreneur are better described as helping out or simply performing what they consider an integral element of their household life. The abstract and impersonal language associated with work does not apply to them. Outsiders may consider such situations exploitative. This position, however, ignores the actor's point of view and the meanings that are endemic to the social realities under investigation.

The Potential for Success or Failure

The typical Greek-American business is small but quite successful. The earnings from it afford the entrepreneur and his family a comfortable but still frugal life-style. More importantly, the business provides for the settlement (*apokatastasis*) of children and, given the comparatively rapid intergenerational mobility of Greek Americans, appears to be quite successful in this respect. Greek-American entrepreneurs tend to achieve the tangible goals for which they became self-employed and are generally content with the rewards of their work.

A major factor behind this success story is the strong work ethic of Greek immigrants. The long, hard workdays may imply a certain masochism to the outsider, but they are financially rewarding to the immigrant entrepreneur. Financial success becomes an ethical imperative to the Greek immigrant, which partly explains his willingness to work long days and to perform such menial tasks as washing dishes and sweeping floors.

An economist might say that the profits generated by a Greek-American business are simply a factor of longer hours. Thus, the businesses cannot be considered technically or economically efficient. Indeed, efficiency in the Western management sense may not be a component of Greek-American businesses; this does not make them any less successful. Formal rationality, the dominant orientation in Western business and bureaucracy, is foreign to the Greek economic ethos, which precludes viewing the domain of work in an impersonal and formalistic manner. The Greek-American way of doing business may not be rationally efficient, but it is definitely profitable. Relying on family members means cheaper and more reliable labor.

The personalistic-familistic character of Greek-American businesses tends to thwart possibilities of expansion, cooperation, or both. Greek-American small business people acknowledge that they could be more successful if they cooperated with relatives or coethnics, but they are not willing to sacrifice personal control of their business. They choose to remain small.

Comparative Cultural Advantage in Small Business

The ethnic group that appears to be the most comparable to Greek-Americans is that of southern Italian-Americans.[3] The latter came to this country at the same time as the Greeks, with premigration experiences that, excluding the economic ethos of the two groups, are similar. Greek and Italian immigrants were primarily peasants with little formal education or skills that could be put to immediate use in the American economy. But, whereas first-generation Greek-Americans generally followed a path toward ethnic enterprise, their Italian counterparts were more likely to develop a working-class culture and remain in factory employment. Italians participated in a subsistence agriculture and did not possess the commercial skills and orientations characteristic of Greek peasants. Also important, however, is the southern Italian ethos, which places greater emphasis on familial solidarity and "ingroup loyalty and conformity to established standards of personal behavior" rather than individual mobility and advancement to the middle class (Gans 1982, 27). This ingroup loyalty and conformity, I suggest, prevents the Italian immigrant from perceiving ethnic entrepreneurialism as a viable occupational option. Starting a business implies being on one's own, which is precisely what the Italian ethos stifles. As a result, first-generation Italian-Americans created communities with a strong working-class orientation and were rather suspicious of the U.S. educational system, which could provide their children with a better chance for socioeconomic mobility. What Herbert Gans found regarding the Italians of the West End in Boston, whom he generally considers representative of all Italian immigrants to America, is instructive. Gans (1982, 31) writes: "Since West Enders reject the middle class . . . those who seek to rise into it must do so either as individuals or as individual family units. Moreover, since no middle-class culture exists among West Enders, the mobile have to model themselves on outsiders. As a result, they must detach themselves from relatives and old friends and are often rejected by these." This Italian pattern contrasts sharply with the experience of Greek immigrant communities. From the early stages of their existence, they emphasized advancement into the middle class and were an infertile ground for the development of a working-class mentality. For the Greeks, individual mobility has always been highly regarded; it was not thought to damage familial or communal considerations. Evidence suggests, in fact, that for Greek-Americans, socioeconomic mobility improves intergenerational familial relations and enhances one's standing in the community.

The Greek economic ethos has a strong propensity for entrepreneurialism, whereas its southern Italian counterpart possesses the opposite quality, that is, it is not conducive to, or is at least indifferent to, the development of small business. As far as ethnic entrepreneurialism is concerned, Greek immigrants have a comparative cultural advantage over southern Italian immigrants. Greeks, of course, are not the only ethnic group with such a cultural advantage; it is characteristic of almost all traditional middleman minorities. The entrepreneurialism of groups such as the Jews, Armenians, Chinese, and Lebanese can be partly explained by reference to class characteristics and premigration experience in business. But this entrepreneurial propensity can also be traced to the transplanted cultural endowments of these groups. Evidence suggests that elements of the economic ethos of traditionally middleman groups—such as strong familism, emphasis on individual mobility, and commercial orientation—appear to be instrumental in the constitution of the middleman experience. The genesis of the economic ethos of particular middleman groups can be traced to diverse factors (for example, although Greek religion appears to be rather inconsequential vis-à-vis the entrepreneurialism of Greeks, the same cannot be said about Confucianism and its role in the economic culture of the overseas Chinese). The general pattern in the experience of all these groups is similar—one may indeed consider this the common middleman pattern. Thus, the different economic ethos under investigation can be seen as functional equivalents vis-à-vis the development of ethnic entrepreneurialism. The commonalities in the experience of groups as diverse as the Greeks and the Chinese suggest that what is unique about the economic culture of any particular middleman group is not a single element but a constellation of elements—many of which are shared by these groups.

Given the conventional neglect of culture, the notion of a comparative cultural advantage does not refer to the possession of concrete occupational skills that may immediately give members of an ethnic group a clear advantage—what might be called a technical advantage—in appropriating entrepreneurial opportunities. Most of the Greek peasants who emigrated to America were not equipped for particular jobs that required specialized skill and know-how. What these people brought with them were diffuse or generic skills. Although not immediately transferable to the American economic scene, these skills allowed them to undertake whatever enterprise they happened to acquire experience in. These diffuse skills may be seen as cultural capital and must be differentiated from assets and abilities that derive from one's social class, occupation, or training.

The Transformation of the Greek into the Greek-American

The Intensification of Economic Life

By intensification of economic life, I refer to a basic phenomenon that emerges in Greek-American communities, gives Greek-American economic culture a quality lacking from that of mainland Greece, and has profound consequences. The Greek immigrant's role as an economic actor acquires increasing importance in the development of his identity and self-understanding. It becomes the paramount mode of his existence. Generally, a Greek-American's honor depends on his economic life and its relative success or failure. Such success or failure is an important part of the sociological locus for the production of what Weber (1976) calls "social premiums" in Greek society. In the case of Greek-Americans, however, it acquires even greater significance and becomes the predominant arena in which one proves one's moral and ontological worth.

Both Greek-Americans and mainland Greeks consider the former to be better workers (*kaliteroi douleutes*) than the latter. Both groups agree that Greek-Americans work harder and for longer hours, more reliably and responsibly, and are more willing to perform menial and undignified tasks. The owner's restaurant or grocery store becomes the center of his existence, often more so than the house, which traditionally is the main locus of the Greek's life-world. Greek-American entrepreneurs constantly worry about their business and insist that this is not the case with their counterparts in Greece. This centrality of work means that Greek-American entrepreneurs have less unwork-related time to spend with their families. This is apparently the only thing they regret about their lives—they do not seem to mind the many hours or the constant worries.

The differences in the intensity of the two economic cultures are also evident in their physiognomy. A mainland Greek and a Greek-American in the same type of work conduct themselves differently in work-related matters. The Greek-American restaurateur spends more hours at the restaurant, often seems to work harder than his employees, has fewer people working for him, and seems unable to get work off his mind. He does not indulge in siestas or coffee breaks, nor does he engage in leisurely talk about politics and other matters like his mainland Greek counterpart.

The Greek immigrant to America is primarily an economic animal. He emigrated purely from economic motives, and this original act seems to stamp his whole existence. What Greek Americans and mainland Greeks have to say about this is instructive: they [we] come here to make money and they [we] work like slaves. This is usually said by Greeks to diminish Greek-Americans and by Greek-Americans to express pride and a sense of accomplishment.

That Greek-Americans are better workers than mainland Greeks is linked to the socioeconomic context in which they operate. The former's is more rewarding than the latter's. Undeniably, more opportunities for economic advancement exist in the United States than in Greece—something that Greek-Americans and mainland Greeks are aware of. The entrepreneurial potential of the Greek economic ethos that flourishes in almost all parts of the Greek diaspora has become stifled in mainland Greece. A variety of factors, ranging from political instability and war to a lucrative system in which government jobs are obtained through political favors, accounts for this difference. The family is the basic structural unit of the Greek economy, but the state also plays a role in it, and the conventional wisdom suggests that this Greek "socialism" is responsible for the country's economic woes. An extensive and inefficient bureaucracy is incapable of coordinating Greek economic affairs. Although everyone condemns this situation, almost everyone benefits, directly or indirectly, from government jobs. Short workdays allow government employees to have a second job, usually at a family business. Securing such a job for one's child is one of the best ways parents can settle their children. That Greek-Americans generally have no such access to government jobs in America is another factor leading to the intensification of economic life that is characteristic of Greek-American communities. Greek immigrants cannot rely on securing government jobs and benefits; thus, entrepreneurial achievement becomes more important. The intensification of economic life appears to be a direct consequence of the disappearance of politics as a means for furthering one's *synferon* (interest of the household). Any further elaboration of these themes would require more detailed data and analysis, and is beyond the scope of the present study. Clearly, however, although the form of mainland Greece's economic culture is not conducive to the development of an entrepreneurial spirit, that spirit manifests itself in societies with a different economic form.

A Parallel Process of Puritanization

Puritanization is an umbrella term that I use to refer to a number of processes accompanying the intensification of economic life.[4] Most of these processes are closely interlinked with the intensification of economic life, but some can be traced to dynamics related to the existence of Greek-Americans as immigrants, and, thus, to their marginal status.

This puritanization involves a social and political conservatism, a more ascetic life-style with less emphasis on literary and artistic pursuits, an expanded role for the family and church, and a more conventional morality, with less tolerance for bohemian life-styles.

Social and Political Conservatism. Greek-Americans are, for the most part, socially and politically conservative. Moskos (1989, 106) refers to the "conservative ethos" of Greek-America: "As imprecise as the term conservative is, it does characterize the ideological bent of most Greek Americans. To call Greek Americans conservative, however, refers not to party identity, not to a coherent body of ideas, but rather to an attitude of mind—a powerful sense of conventional mores, a distaste for confrontational politics, a wish to enjoy the fruits of one's labor, a betterment through individualistic actions, and a suspicion of collective steps for social improvement. Greek Americans search not for a better world, but for a better life." This aspect of the Greek-American ethos became evident in the interviews conducted for this study. My respondents placed great value on individual achievement and responsibility; they vehemently opposed any state intervention in the economic affairs of its citizens. Not surprisingly, they had a strong antiwelfare sentiment and considered the expansion of the welfare-state detrimental to the health of U.S. society and economy. My respondents were firmly convinced that most welfare recipients do not really need government assistance and simply take advantage of the system. They proudly pointed out that very few Greek-Americans are on welfare and attributed this to the Greek's traditional values of independence and individual responsibility.

A conservative ideology with a strong emphasis on self-reliance was a significant part of the culture of modern Greece, but in the period following the Greek civil war (1944–49), the Greek ethos underwent a process of radicalization, which has become evident in both the political culture and the more general contours of Greek life. As a result of these changes, which were missed by many Greek immigrants, mainland Greeks and Greek-Americans have begun to grow apart in terms of their political ideology and the way they think about society and the role of individuals therein. The mainland Greek is more susceptible to socialist ideals and leftist politics, expects more from the state, and views conventional mores with a more open mind. The electoral win of PASOK and its eight years in power put an effective end to a tradition of political domination by the right and brought this radicalization of Greek political culture to the surface. Most Greek-Americans have been hostile to these developments in mainland Greece, and, as Moskos put it, there has been a "growing rift between mainstream Greek Americans and the new mood in Greece" (1989, 168).

The radicalization of mainland Greek culture was the result of various significant transformations, such as internal migration and rapid urbanization, that Greece underwent in the period following the civil war. It became evident with George Papandreou and continues up to the present. The process acquired a faster pace when the military dictatorship (1967–74) ended. Seven years of political repression changed Greek society and culture. The dictatorship of the colonels was centered around a strong anticommunist ideology and the espousal of traditional values concerning Greek family and religion. Not surprisingly, then, with the fall of the military regime, the sentiments and ideals it embodied were weakened. An important feature of the post-1974 developments was that for the first time in Greek political history the forces of the left were allowed full participation in the mainstream political system. The left acquired a respectability it had not had before. The possibility of true political reconciliation exists between the forces of the left and the right, whose animosities, dating back to the Civil War, have not yet been healed. Whether the defeat of PASOK in 1989 signifies a reversal of this radicalization process is not yet clear. Very likely, this radicalization has been only a temporary phenomenon, the result of sudden change and upheaval. As things settle down and Greek society achieves a new equilibrium (and the security of being a member of the European Community), Greek politics may well regain its emphasis on conservative ideology.

Greek-Americans, however, have not been in tune with the radicalization of Greek politics, and their political outlook seems to be more conservative than that of mainland Greeks. Greek-Americans were generally in favor of the military rule in Greece and hostile toward the first socialist government. The claim, often heard among leftist mainland Greeks, that the political culture of Greek-Americans contains a strong fascist element is unfounded. Greek-Americans cannot be thought of as fascists— a characterization that is offered in political discussions in the Greek parliament and in coffeehouses—in any sensible meaning of the term. The affinity between Greek-American political culture and the ideology of the 1967–74 military dictatorship lies in the Greek colonels' attempt to emphasize certain traditional aspects of Greek culture—for example, family and the Orthodox faith—which are important to Greek-Americans. However, Greek-Americans are unsympathetic to the idea of an interventionist state and presumably would oppose the colonels' efforts to regulate such aspects of daily life as the length of skirts and the breaking of plates in traditional Greek music places. Greek-Americans' criticism of the PASOK socialist rule focuses on the interventionist character of socialist ideology, such as nationalization of the economy and higher taxes. The self-made Greek-American entrepreneur does not have any sympathy for socialist sentiments. This is the essence of the social and political conservatism of Greek-America.

Researchers of Greece have noted a "hyperpoliticization" of the political culture of modern Greece (Mouzelis 1992; Tsoukalas 1983, 1985); Greek-America appears to be markedly different in this respect. Basically, this "hyperpoliticization of the political phenomenon" has been linked to the "hypertrophy" of the modern Greek state (Tsoukalas 1983, 28). But the concept can illuminate more general issues concerning the Greek political culture, such as how individuals view and understand the political process and its place in the social world they construct. Modern Greeks have a political sensitivity—evident in, among other things, the frequent *diadiloseis* (demonstrations), *diamartyries* (protests), and strikes that often disrupt daily life, from the operation of buses and universities to the collection of trash—that is not seen as often in other Western countries. This sensitivity can be linked to a belief that the political process is significantly consequential vis-à-vis the lives of individuals. This belief gradually disappears from the conceptual repertoire of the Greek-American immigrant who "searches for a better life" as an individual not for a better world as a *zoon politikon* (social animal). The Greek immigrants' individualism necessarily leads to a devaluation of the political phenomenon, and this underpoliticization differentiates them from their more hyperpoliticized compatriots who never emigrated. In addition, mainland Greeks have high stakes in the mainstream political system (such as jobs and political favors), whereas Greek immigrants have a marginal place in the American political system. For Greek-American immigrants, politics is no longer a means for the advancement of the *synferon* of the family; therefore, they have to rely almost exclusively on their own labor—the weakening of politics, it can be argued, is closely interlinked with the intensification of economic life.

The decreasing importance of politics occurs simultaneously with the increasing importance of economics, and both are indicative of the socioeconomic adjustment of Greek immigrants. The first-generation Greek-American small businessman—who can be seen as the prototypical Greek-American—strongly believes that what matters is what the individual himself does and that government ought to have little to do with how individuals construct a meaningful existence for themselves. Many of my Greek-American respondents thought that one of the basic reasons the economy of Greece is plagued with serious problems is because citizens get preoccupied with politics at the expense of hard and dedicated work. For Greek immigrants, political activity is almost always—with the exception, of course, of situations such as a Greek-American candidate for president and the promotion of national issues like the Macedonian dispute or Graeco-Turkish relations—seen as an expenditure of time and energy that can only come at the expense of more serious things, such as working and tending to everyday needs. Greek-Americans, moreover, appear to be almost outraged with the excessive politicization of mainland Greek students who "have much more to gain by going to classes and studying than from expressing political opinions." Their own children, Greek immigrant parents are proud to say, are more "serious," and "less politicized." The American-born generations, who exhibit comparatively rapid rates of socioeconomic mobility, do get involved in the American political system, but this is seen as entirely different from active political participation in Greece. In the eyes of the immigrant generation, the second-generation Greek-American congressman, senator, or presidential candidate, is a "professional" and a "good manager"—in contrast to their Greek counterparts whom Greek-Americans would usually describe as "crooks" and "charlatans." Furthermore, and this is the key issue here, Greek-American politicians provide ample evidence that "the Greeks are really making it in America."

Other puritanizing processes differentiate Greek-Americans and mainland Greeks, and give the former a distinct, truly hybrid, identity. The social and political conservatism of Greek-Americans constitutes the most consequential element of the puritanization of the Greek diaspora and subsequent ethnicity in America, but other sociocultural developments are of interest to the sociologist studying Greek-America. These developments include an expanded role for the family and the church, a more conventional and traditionally Greek morality, a more ascetic lifestyle, and a considerable reduction of the sociological locus of bohemian, as well as literary, elements. Whereas these nascent and sui generis features of Greek-American ethnicity are clearly related to the social and political conservatism endemic to the socioeconomic adaptation of Greeks in America, their genesis is also linked to the more general phenomena of the experience and marginality of immigrants. Perhaps this analysis of the culturally specific experience of Greek Americans will improve our understanding of the cultural aspects of immigrant life, a more general problematic that is often forgotten in the mainstream social scientific literature.

Literary and Artistic Production. The Greek immigrant culture in America has less social space for literary and artistic production than does mainland Greek culture. Considering that most Greek immigrants were formerly peasants, this should not come as a surprise. However, additional factors are pertinent to this issue and are closely linked with the economic intensification of Greek-American culture. As the Greek-American's economic instincts strengthen, his artistic and literary instincts weaken. This refers to a *general* trend in Greek-American culture; the author is well aware that Greek-America has produced significant literary and artistic figures. People such as Maria Callas and Elias Kazan are Greek-American, but it is not as Greek-Americans that they made their careers: the former was the *Greek* Divina, the latter an *American* movie giant, and both existed in environments far removed from Greek-American experience. Greek-Americans, even when they have achieved an economic position that allows them to support art and literature in their own communities, are reluctant to do so. Generally, they prefer to contribute to the development of educational and scientific pursuits. Greek-Americans have more respect for the scientist than for the artist, something that Greek-American intellectuals—who are part of the Greek-American experience—continually complain about. Greek-American immigrant artists find themselves in a milieu that often seems indifferent, if not hostile, to artistic pursuits. To a considerable degree, this is because the typical Greek-American is so preoccupied with his business that he simply has neither the time nor the energy for such pursuits. And when he finds the time or energy, he usually prefers to turn to the mainland Greek artistic and literary scene, which is well established and continues to have an audience in the Greek diaspora. Thus, the first-generation Greek-American audience—an audience that is limited and slow to develop—in pursuit of what may be called high culture can easily turn to the available production in the mainland and overlook its indigenous producers.

The Greek-American immigrant gradually and slowly develops a crystallized identity; he initially views himself as simply Greek, and, therefore, feels closer to the homeland culture. This sentiment is evident not only in the consumers but also in the producers of high culture. Not surprisingly, then, first-generation Greek-American poets do not consider themselves Greek-American *logotechnes* (producers of literature), but Greeks who write in America. Greece is still their true *patrida* (homeland), and it is as Greeks that they try to understand their experiences in America. The arena in which they try to achieve recognition is not just Greek-America, but mainland Greece. Although it is as a Greek that the first-generation Greek-American writes, his themes are alien to the cultural tastes of mainland Greece. Moreover, the poets and, more generally, the intellectuals of mainland Greece are reluctant, if not actively opposed to, accepting Greeks of the diaspora into their ranks. Ever since the virtual disappearance of some traditional centers of the Greek Diaspora, such as Smyrna, Alexandria, and Constantinople, Athens has claimed intellectual hegemony over all the modern Greek nation, and it often gives the appearance of completely neglecting the Greek diaspora. If the Athens-based literary establishment recognized Constantine Cavafis only at his death, one can easily imagine the difficulties of first-generation Greek-American poets in gaining recognition from Greece. First-generation Greek-American *logotechnes*—and the same applies to other artists—find themselves in a precarious and marginal position that may often stifle their work. They reside in a community that ignores their presence, and they seek recognition from an audience that is not only thousands of miles away but also indifferent to their work.

That Greek-American communities develop this indifference toward literary and artistic production, and, thus, a certain anti-intellectualism, is related to the strong emphasis on education and a respect for academics and scientists. Professional education (business, law, medicine) and the hard sciences are especially valued. In mainland Greece *logotechnia* is held in higher esteem than science; in Greek-America the reverse is true. This, I suggest, is linked to the Greek immigrant's attempt to become part of the American milieu and gain recognition from it. Upwardly mobile Greek immigrants prefer that their children—who will, after all, be more American than Greek—become doctors, lawyers, or established academics, and not poets or actors. Artistic types do eventually appear among American-born Greek-Americans, but they are significantly different from their immigrant counterparts. They write in English and address themselves to the general American public. That the children of immigrants excel in these areas clearly disproves the comment—often heard—among mainland Greeks and first-generation Greek-American *logotechnes*—that Greek-Americans are simply "backward" and "uncultured" peasants-turned-restauranteurs.

The reduction in social space for artistic production was one of the main issues at a panel discussion on Greek-American literature and its problems at the Second Annual Greek Studies Conference at Hellenic College in October 1990. Two of the better-known first-generation Greek-American poets talked about "the indifference of the coethnics for literature" (*i adiaforia ton omogenon yia tin logotechnia*) and commented on the "indifference of the people in charge of immigrant organizations" (*i adiaforia ton armodion*). "The Greeks in America who write, the 'logotechnes,' " as one of the poets put it, "get no respect from the Greek-American community, the only exception being the 'logotechnes' who hold academic positions."[5]

The decreased significance of logotechnia in Greek-American immigrant culture is recognizable as a puritanizing development, when one considers that the puritan ethos has traditionally displayed a certain hostility toward the arts and literary pursuits. Puritan communities have an "almost complete lack of belles lettres" (Weber 1990, 274), but they have traditionally been supportive of scientific endeavors.

An Expanded Role for Family and Church. An integral part of the puritanization of Greek-America is the increased significance of the family and the church. Greek immigrants find themselves in an alien environment (*xenitia*). As a result, their families and the Greek Orthodox Church acquire a place and a significance that they did not have in mainland Greece. The Greek immigrant can no longer rely on the neighborhood, the local community, or the peer group—institutions that play a significant role in mainland Greece; thus, the strengthening of family and church ties would appear to be inevitable. The Greek-American church has a much more grass roots character than its mainland Greek counterpart and plays a more significant role in the life of its members. The church is the ethnic institution par excellence, and most researchers of Greek-America find that among the immigrant generation ethnicity and religion are almost inseparable. The Greek-American priest often achieves the character of an "ethnarch," a leader who is simultaneously an ethnic and a religious figure. As the role of the church gains significance, the Greek American may claim that this leads to increased religiousness. Whether this is true in a spiritual sense is not subject to empirical evidence, but the institutional centrality of the Greek church in America is apparent.

Church and family are also perceived as guardians of the Greekness of Greek-American youth. Greek immigrants find themselves in an environment in which their Greekness, and more especially that of their children, faces severe and often inescapable threats. Thus, the Greek immigrant clings to these bastions of Greekness—family and church—with an intensity unknown in the modern mainland. Greek-American immigrant parents are concerned with how to maintain their roots and the Greekness of their children, and the Greek-American family acquires some of the roles traditionally held by the nation or the village. The church is where the immigrant's children learn Greek and the history of the homeland; it is the institution that represents him in the wider public. As one of my respondents put it, the church is the mind of Greek America; the family is its heart. I suggest that an inevitable result of the increased role of the family and the church is that Greek Americans develop a more traditional, more conservative, and more regulated mentality than mainland Greeks. They become, in other words, more socially and politically conservative. The complexity of the social factors at work in these dynamics of Greek-American social life, however, is beyond the scope of this study.

The Greek immigrant clings to his institutions in the form they had at the time he left Greece. As a result, the Greekness of Greek-America often seems to be frozen in time. The first-generation Greek-American clings to traditional values of the homeland with greater fervor than does his compatriot who did not leave Greece. To a significant degree, this traditionalism—which can be observed in the experience of other ethnic groups—is a matter of cultural survival and of preserving a clear sense of identity and belonging for immigrants (and their offspring). Although the defenses of Greek immigrants against Americanization (and, thus, the preservation of their Greekness) are often successful, some erosion and transfiguration of the Greekness of Greek America is inescapable. Immigrant parents know that their American-born children will be much less Greek than they are, and evidence suggests that, with the third, and even more so the fourth, generation, Greek-American ethnicity acquires an increasingly symbolic character. In this, Greek-Americans are similar to other white ethnics. Some Greek-Americans claim that the erosion of Greekness often comes *as a reaction to* the conservatism of the mainstream institutions of the ethnic community, but this claim has not been substantiated. A certain erosion of Greekness is, of course, inevitable.

Conventional Morality and the Displacement of Bohemian Elements. Another feature of the puritanization of Greek-America is a more conventional and definitely stricter morality than in mainland Greece. This is especially evident in how Greek-Americans think about courtship and sexuality. The Greek immigrants interviewed for this study vehemently opposed any "dating" on the part of their teenage children, and stressed that their "girls" are "better girls" (*kaliteres kopelles,* which in this case basically refers to the virginity of unmarried women) than what one generally finds in mainland Greece. The situation in Greece, they believe, has changed considerably and things are not as they used to be when they were growing up there. "Nowadays, Greek girls do not stay at home, and are becoming more and more like American girls." Greek-American girls, on the other hand, have kept the traditional Greek ways and are considered better marriage prospects for Greek-American men. Moreover, a Greek-American man is considered a better marriage partner than a mainland Greek, who, Greek-Americans think, is more likely to be unfaithful to or otherwise abuse his wife. Mainland Greeks, on the other hand, tend to view the Greek-American attitude as backward and outdated. "This is how Greece was fifty years ago," they say, "and this is how Greek immigrants in America are now." These perceptions reflect the growing rift between the two cultures, which arises from the sociocultural adaptation of Hellenic existence in America.

The ethos that gradually develops among Greek-Americans becomes increasingly hostile toward certain bohemian and marginal elements of Greek culture. In Greek-America, for example, there has been a displacement—and one that is more pronounced than the analogous process in the mainland—of the social type known as the *rembetis,* or *mangas.* Elias Petropoulos, perhaps the most insightful ethnographer of Greek marginality, defines the *rembetis* as "the man who has a distinctive life-style outside the mainstream of society. The *rembetis* showed his contempt for the establishment in every possible way: he did not marry, he did

116

not embrace his girlfriend, he did not wear a collar and tie, he walked shakingly, he had a deadly hatred for policemen, he never used an umbrella, helped the weak, smoked hashish, he considered prison a sign of braveness, etc." (Petropoulos 1990, 10). The Greek-American ethos, with its emphasis on family, church life, and economic achievement, has much less tolerance for the *rembetis,* who is the embodiment of marginality (and a conscious repudiation of bourgeois morality). Greek-American life moves increasingly toward the mainstream and away from the life-style of the *rembetiko.*

The Greek-American acumen for small business can be explained by reference to the transplanted economic ethos of Greek-Americans and the various transformations that it undergoes in American society. The economic culture that emerges in the transformation of the Greek into the Greek-American is clearly an offspring of the economic culture of Greece. It is also significantly different. The economic ethos of first-generation Greek-Americans exhibits an intensification of economic life and a parallel process of puritanization, both of which are conducive to the development and successful operation of small businesses. This new economic ethos provides Greek immigrants with a comparative cultural advantage in ethnic entrepreneurialism in America.

Notes

I thank Brigitte Berger, Peter Berger, Marilyn Halter, Valerie Michaels, and Silvia Pedraza for reading and commenting on earlier drafts of this paper.

1. This essay is based on data collected for a dissertation entitled "Ethnic Entrepreneurialism, Social Mobility, and Embourgeoisement: The Formation and Intergenerational Evolution of Greek-American Economic Culture" (Boston University, 1993). An economic culture approach to Greek-American ethnic entrepreneurialism investigates "the social, political, and cultural matrix" within which the economic conduct (or economic form) of Greek-American family entrepreneurs and their economically relevant values and culture (or economic ethos) are constructed (Berger 1986, 7). The essential building blocks for the construction of this theoretical model can be found in the work of Max Weber (1978, 1987, 1990) and Peter Berger who has coined the term "economic culture." For a more extensive theoretical elaboration of these issues see Mavratsas (1993).

2. Greek-Americans are aware of the differences that gradually develop between themselves and mainland Greeks and see some of them as causes of their socioeconomic success in America.

3. The term "comparative cultural advantage" was coined by Peter Berger in discussions at the Institute for the Study of Economic Culture.

4. The puritanization discussed here is a concept that arises out of comparisons

between Greek-Americans and mainland Greeks; similar patterns also develop among other middleman minorities such as Jews and Cubans. This point was raised by the comments of Silvia Pedaza 1 May 1992.

5. The poets referred to are R. Pagoulatou, R. Capatos, and E. Paidousi.

References

Berger, Peter. 1986. *The Capitalist Revolution: Fifty Propositions about Prosperity, Equality, and Liberty*. New York: Basic Books.

Burghess, Thomas. 1913. *Greeks in America*. Boston: Sherman, French.

Campbell, J. K. 1974. *Honour, Family, and Patronage: A Study of Institutions and Moral Values in a Greek Mountain Community*. New York: Oxford University Press.

Fratoe, Frank, and Ronald Meeks. 1985. *Business Participation Rates of the 50 Largest U.S. Ancestry Groups: Preliminary Report*. Washington, D.C.: U.S. Department of Commerce, Research Division, Office of Advocacy, Research, and Information, June.

Friedl, Ernestine. 1964. *Vasilika: A Village in Modern Greece*. New York: Holt, Rinehart and Winston.

Gans, Herbert. 1982. *The Urban Villagers: Group and Class in the Life of Italian-Americans* (updated and expanded edition). New York: Free Press.

Light, Ivan. 1984. "Immigrant and Ethnic Enterprise in North America." *Ethnic and Racial Studies* 7, no. 2: 195–216.

Loizos, Peter. 1975. *The Greek Gift: Politics in a Cypriot Village*. New York: St. Martin's.

Lovell-Troy, Lawrence. 1980. "Clan Structure and Economic Activity: The Case of Greeks in Small Business Enterprise." In *Self-Help in Urban America*, edited by Scott Cummings. Port Washington, N.Y.: Kennikat Press.

———. 1981. "Ethnic Occupational Structures: Greeks in the Pizza Business." *Ethnicity* 8: 82–95.

Malafouris, Bobby. 1948. *Ellines tis Amerikis* (Greeks of America). New York: Author.

Mavratsas, Caesar. 1993. "Ethnic Entrepreneurialism, Social Mobility, and Embourgeoisement: The Formation and Intergenerational Evolution of Greek-American Economic Culture." Ph.D. diss., Boston University.

McNeil, William. 1978. *The Metamorphosis of Greece since World War II*. Chicago: University of Chicago Press.

Monos, Dimitri. 1976. *Upward Mobility: Assimilation and the Achievements of Greeks in the United States with Special Emphasis on Boston and Philadelphia*. Ph.D. diss., University of Pennsylvania.

Moskos, Charles. 1982. "Georgakas on Greek-Americans: A Response by Charles Moskos." *Journal of the Hellenic Diaspora* 14, nos. 1 and 2: 55–61.

———. 1989. *Greek-Americans: Struggle and Success*, 2d ed. New Brunswick, N.J.: Transaction.

Papaioannou, George. 1985. *The Odyssey of Hellenism in America*. Thessaloniki, Greece: Patriarchal Institute for Patristic Studies.

Pedraza, Silvia. 1992. Conversation with author, 1 May.

Peristiany, J. G. ed. 1984. *Honour and Shame: The Values of Mediterranean Society*. Chicago: University of Chicago Press.

Petropoulos, Elias. 1990. *Rembetology* (Rembetologia). Athens, Greece: Kedros.

Rosen, Bernard. 1959. "Race, Ethnicity, and the Achievement Syndrome," *Sociological Review* 24, no. 1: 47–60.

Saloutos, Theodore. *The Greeks in the United States.* Cambridge: Harvard University Press.

Sanders, Irwin. 1962. *Rainbow in the Rock: The People of Rural Greece.* Cambridge: Harvard University Press.

Scourby, Alice. 1984. *The Greek-Americans.* Boston: Twayne.

Tavouchis, Nicholas. 1972. *Family and Mobility among Greek-Americans.* Athens, Greece: National Center of Social Research.

Tsoukalas, Constantine. 1983. *Social Development and State: The Formation of Public Space in Greece* (Kinoniki Anaptixi ke Kratos: I Singrotisi tou Dimosiou Chorou stin Ellada). Athens, Greece: Themelio.

——. 1985. "Thoughts on the Social Role of State Employment in Greece." In *The State in Peripheral Capitalism.* Athens: Exantas.

Vlachos, Evan C. 1968. *The Assimilation of Greeks in the United States.* Athens: National Center of Social Research.

Weber, Max. 1978. *Economy and Society: An Outline of Interpretive Sociology,* edited by Guenther Roth and Claus Wittich. Berkeley: University of California Press.

——. 1987. *General Economic History,* translated by Frank H. Knight, with an introduction by Ira J. Cohen. New Brunswick, N.J.: Transaction.

——. 1990. *The Protestant Ethic and the Spirit of Capitalism,* translated by Talcott Parsons. London: Unwin Hyman.

Zotos, Stephanos. 1976. *Hellenic Presence in America.* Wheaton, Ill.: Pilgrimage.

Chapter 6

A Todos Les Llamo Primo
(I Call Everyone Cousin):
The Social Basis
for Latino Small Businesses

Peggy Levitt

Puerto Ricans and Dominicans are less likely than their foreign-born counterparts to own small businesses. In 1980, the average business participation rate among the 50 largest foreign-born ancestry groups was 48.9 compared to 10.6 and 14.6 among Puerto Ricans and Dominicans, respectively (Fratoe and Meeks 1985).[1] Whereas 6 percent of the population in the United States was self-employed, only 1.7 percent of all Hispanics, including 0.7 percent of all Puerto Ricans owned their own businesses (Waldinger, Aldrich, and Ward 1990). Self-employment rates among Latinos in Boston appear to be consistent with these trends. Between 1969 and 1982, less than 1 percent of the Latino population owned their own businesses (U.S. Department of Commerce 1971a, 1971b, 1974, 1979, 1982, 1985, 1990, 1992). In 1985, only 5 percent of all the self-employed residents in Boston were Hispanic (Boston Redevelopment Authority 1987).

In this chapter, I argue that an unfavorable opportunity structure and Latino group characteristics contribute to these modest rates of small business development.[2] A small group of entrepreneurs combine ethnic and class resources to overcome these barriers and open businesses serving a primarily ethnic market (Light and Bonacich 1988). But the same resources that make business ownership possible also seem to create inherent constraints to performance and growth. In general, Latino businesses generate only modest profits and few jobs, constituting economic survival strategies rather than the springboards to economic advancement that entrepreneurship has been for other immigrant groups in the past.

Two findings from this study, however, call into question some ideas in good currency about mobility and progress. First, in addition to their economic function, the Latino small business sector plays a crucial institutional role in providing for and integrating its community. Latino businesses ensure a base level of stability and well-being, thus laying the foundation from which economic development can begin. Second, the business owners in this study are seemingly comfortable with their business performance. This suggests that some Latino entrepreneurs may be guided by a notion of prosperity and growth that emphasizes stability and self-preservation over large-scale advancement and accumulation.

Study Methodology

The findings outlined below are based on thirty-four in-depth interviews with twenty-six Puerto Rican and Dominican business owners (eleven Puerto Rican, and fifteen Dominican) and eight community leaders and long-time Latino residents; interviews were conducted between January and July 1991. I identified store owners using an informal, snowball sampling strategy. A Puerto Rican and Dominican leader introduced me to a group of business owners who then led me to other potential respondents. Although I interviewed business owners from each of the largest Latino commercial districts in Boston and Cambridge, the sample is not representative of all Latino businesses in the area.[3]

The types of businesses included in the study are summarized in table 1.[4] In general, Latino businesses sell retail goods and services. They have been open an average of 7.76 years, ranging from 3 months to 22 years. Sixteen businesses started less than 5 years ago. The businesses employed an average of 1.8 full-time employees; many also relied on part-time unpaid assistance from family members and friends. Most businesses sold ethnic products to a primarily Latino clientele. Three businesses produced small quantities of garments for sale in their own stores; only one business manufactured clothing to sell to other retailers. I asked business owners to describe the history of their business, its daily operations, and the Latino business community in general. Most interviews lasted from one to two hours. I conducted approximately 65 percent of the interviews in Spanish. Approximately 50 percent were taped.

Boston's Latino community also includes Cubans and Central and

Table 1. Types of Businesses in the Study

Retail			*Service*	
Type	*Number*		*Type*	*Number*
Botanica[a]	2		Barbershop	1
Bridal Shop	1		Catering	2
Clothing	4		Immigrant Services[b]	1
Furniture	1		Radio Station	1
Gift Shop	1		Restaurant	1
Grocery, large	2		Tailor	1
Grocery, small	3			
Plastic Slipcovers	2			
Record Store	1			
Video	1			
Video/Clothing	1			

[a] Sells religious articles and medicinal herbs.
[b] Prepares immigration papers, insurance, and income taxes.

South Americans, but this study focuses on Puerto Ricans and Dominicans for several reasons. Puerto Ricans were the first large Latino group to settle in Boston; they are now the largest and most established group here. Dominicans constitute a second significant group; there were 7,938 legal Dominicans in 1990 (U.S. Department of Commerce 1992). Community leaders estimate that the illegal population may be half again that size. An earlier study found that despite sustained fiscal growth and nearly full employment in Massachusetts throughout most of the 1980s, poverty rates among Latinos were twice that of blacks and at least five times greater than the rates among whites (Osterman 1990). Puerto Ricans and Dominicans fared worse than Cubans (the Central and South American sample size was too small to be conclusive). There did not appear to be significant entrepreneurship among South and Central Americans in the Boston area at the time of this study. The migration flow from these areas is still quite small. The Central American community in particular may be disinclined toward entrepreneurship because many people are here either illegally or as political asylum seekers for what they hope will be a brief period.

Throughout this chapter, I use the overarching rubric of Latino to discuss those aspects of business practice that Puerto Ricans and Do-minicans seem to share. There are also important differences between these two groups that this study, because of its small size and the relative newness of the Dominican community, only begins to hint at. I discuss these briefly in the section below.

Small Business Development in Boston

In general, the rate of Latino business development has not kept pace with Latino population growth. Between 1969 and 1989, less than 1 per-cent of all Latinos in Massachusetts owned their own businesses. There were fewer than three hundred Latino-owned businesses within the Boston Standard Metropolitan Statistical Area (SMSA), an estimated twenty-mile area encircling the city (U.S. Department of Commerce 1974, 1979, 1985, 1990).

In 1990, there were 61,995 Latino residents in Boston. Forty-two per-cent were Puerto Rican and 13 percent were Dominican (U.S. Depart-ment of Commerce 1992). In 1987, Hispanics in Boston owned 460 small firms. The 86 firms that employed paid workers reported average annual sales and receipts per firm of $206,000. The 374 firms with no paid em-ployees reported average sales and receipts of $29,000. No data are avail-able by type of firm for businesses located in Boston. Of the 2,616 His-panic-owned firms statewide, however, 54 percent (1,425) were service firms and 16 percent (411) were retail stores (U.S. Department of Com-merce 1990).[5]

The literature on ethnic entrepreneurship explains rates of immigrant small business ownership as a function of a particular group's access to opportunities, their characteristics, and the sociohistorical context that greets them upon their arrival (Pedraza-Bailey and Waldinger 1991; Light and Bonacich 1988). In the following paragraphs, I explore how well this model fits the experience of Latino business owners in Boston.

The original wave of migrants who arrived in Boston in the 1960s were primarily farm workers from rural Puerto Rico. They had neither the language, education, nor capital with which to start small businesses (Piore 1979). The second wave of Puerto Rican migrants began in the 1970s. It consisted primarily of middle-class professionals and semi-professionals who, according to one community leader, "were not inter-ested in entrepreneurship. They had a different idea of what it meant to be upwardly mobile . . . to work as professors, in the social services,

123

Table 2. Self-Employment among Boston Residents, 1985

	Whites	*Blacks*	*Asians*	*Hispanics/ Other Minorities*
% of all self-employed	79	14	2	5
% of ethnic/racial group self-employed	9	5	0	6

Source: Boston Redevelopment Authority, 1987

government jobs. . . . Some looked at owning a store as being a slave." Most of the first Latino business owners in the city were Puerto Ricans and Cubans. During the 1980s, a pattern of ethnic succession occurred whereby these original owners sold their businesses to newly arriving Dominicans and moved out of the area. Because significant numbers of Dominicans began to arrive as recently as 1980, it is difficult to predict what their levels of entrepreneurship will be. Dominicans currently appear to be overrepresented in the small business sector relative to their group size. They own most of the businesses in three of the Latino commercial districts; several families own multiple businesses.

There are several reasons why Dominicans may have higher rates of entrepreneurship than Puerto Ricans:

1. There is some evidence that Dominican migrants in Boston are more educated than their Puerto Rican counterparts. Prior research on Dominican migration to the United States found that Dominicans tend to be young, urban, middle class, skilled workers, or semiprofessionals (Georges 1990; Ugalde, Bean, and Cardenas 1979). Indeed, two-thirds of the Dominican business owners in this study had some university education as opposed to only 36 percent of the Puerto Ricans.
2. Most early Puerto Rican immigrants were single men who came on labor contracts, whereas Dominicans tended to migrate as families, thus creating a built-in labor supply.
3. As citizens, Puerto Ricans have more job opportunities, while some Dominicans' illegal status impedes them from securing certain kinds of employment. Puerto Ricans also have easier access to government

aid programs. Dominicans, then, may be pushed into small business ownership for lack of other options.

4. By the time Dominicans began arriving in Boston, city officials had come to recognize Latinos as an increasingly important constituency. Dominican business owners probably benefited from a system that had been broken in a decade before by Puerto Ricans.

5. Finally, while urban renewal in the 1970s rapidly dispersed the Puerto Rican community from its point-of-arrival in the South End, there has been a fairly stable residential concentration of Latinos in other neighborhoods over the last fifteen years. Early Puerto Rican storeowners did not have access to the critical mass of consumers that Dominican entrepreneurs now enjoy.

Today, most Latinos still lack the skills and resources needed for business development. Latinos in Boston are young, with a median age of only twenty-four (U.S. Department of Commerce 1992). A 1989 study of poverty in the city found that 46 percent of all Latinos had incomes below 125 percent of the federal poverty line. Forty-four percent had not finished high school. Forty-two percent were classified by interviewers as speaking English only fairly or poorly (Osterman 1990). Forty-three percent of all Latino families in Massachusetts in 1990 lived in female-headed households (U.S. Department of Commerce 1992).

The opportunity structure during the 1970s and 1980s did not favor minority small business development. In the 1970s, Massachusetts lost 8 percent of all its manufacturing jobs, at a time when 37 percent of Latinos were employed in manufacturing industries (Melendez 1994; Harrison 1988). The structure of the retail sector was also changing. Between 1960 and 1990 retail sales dropped by $3 billion, and five thousand retail stores closed or moved out of the city (Levine 1991). Would-be business owners faced a shrinking retail market and heightened competition for entrepreneurial opportunities from displaced industrial workers. They also needed to go into businesses that required little start-up capital and in which their ethnic attributes were assets rather than liabilities. Most Latinos opened businesses aimed at the emerging, largely underserved ethnic market.

The Latino community could only support a small number of retail stores. In 1980, there were only thirty-six thousand Latino residents in Boston. Their average annual income was $11,800 (U.S. Department of Commerce 1982). It was difficult for Latinos to expand into the non-ethnic market for several reasons. Most business owners had no contact with the formal banking system. Banks in Boston have since been cited for their record of nonlending to minorities (Massachusetts Commission against Discrimination 1991). Only four business owners had ever participated in a publicly sponsored small business development program. The others either did not know that such resources existed, did not understand how to enroll, or were suspicious of the assistance that was offered. Finally, because Latino businesses were few in number and concentrated in the retail sector, they had limited opportunities to establish the types of coethnic linkages that have given rise to successful enclave economies in other parts of the country (Portes and Manning 1986).

Nevertheless, some Latinos did open businesses and have been successful. Ethnic resources and the ability to mobilize these through ethnic social networks allowed potential business owners to compensate for the unfavorable social context and opportunity structure that greeted them. The following section describes in some detail the way in which Latino entrepreneurs use ethnic resources to acquire capital, information, clients, and labor.

The Social Characteristics of Latino Businesses

Capital

Most of the entrepreneurs in this study went into business with minimal start-up funds, ranging from three thousand to fifteen thousand dollars. Although Latinos have no formal equivalent of the revolving loan associations pivotal to the formation of Korean and Japanese small businesses (Light and Bonacich 1988), more than two-thirds of the business owners in this study got loans from their family and friends. Other sources of funding included personal savings, pension funds, credit card debt, selling merchandise door-to-door, and even the lottery. In some cases, the individuals who loan money are close relatives. In others, they are merely acquaintances who make a loan because the borrower is a coethnic. In one case, Dominican businessmen in New York loaned a video store owner money because his family had a "serious" reputation in his hometown.

These money lenders constitute a quick, low-interest, easily accessible alternative banking system. Only four business owners got actual bank loans; two got personal loans, which they used for business purposes. Business owners generally borrow small amounts from a number of individuals. It is not uncommon to borrow from one to pay back another. In general, no formal papers are exchanged—the borrowers' standing in the community and the assumption that they will want to uphold their status serve as collateral. The interest charged, if any, is often calculated according to the needs of the lender *and* the borrower. In other words, in some cases, money lending is a social service rather than an investment strategy, as this bridal shop owner described:

> I had forty-five dollars in my bank book. She said, that's okay, come and see the store. . . . She said to me I am going to negotiate the price. I said wait a minute, you are going to negotiate the price but where is the money? She said go and call your friends and ask them to lend you money. I got nine thousand dollars lent to me from friends. . . . She said perfect, I will look for more and she got it for me. We bought the store and she said I am going to arrange it so that you don't have to pay that much interest. This person doesn't need this money right now, so they made it as if the person had their money in the bank and I pay it back little by little.

Business Location

Ethnic social networks play an important role in helping business owners identify opportunities and make decisions about business locations. Eight of the nine business owners in the study who purchased already existing businesses bought them from other Latinos. Those that started their own businesses often found out about vacant stores from coethnics. Many business owners chose a particular location because it was close to friends and family members. For example, a clothing store owner and an immigrant services firm owner, both from Bani, the southwestern city where many Dominicans in Boston come from, chose to open their stores in a building owned by two other Banilejos, despite its location off the main thoroughfare in a high-crime neighborhood. They viewed this arrangement as mutually beneficial to both parties—landlords offered the fledgling businesses lower rents and a streamlined leasing process in exchange for a "social security deposit," or a surer guarantee that rents would be paid because their tenants felt a sense of obligation to them.

Because business owners often know one another, information is also exchanged indirectly through informal conversations in bars, bodegas, or on the street: "In the business life of the community, you hear who is lending money. People send offers to one another. They tell me, so-and-so wants to know if you are interested in buying this business. The information network is internal. . . . You don't go looking for information but you talk a lot" (Clothing store owner).

Skills Training and Technical Assistance

The ethnic entrepreneurship literature suggests that prior business experience is an important variable in determining levels of self-employment (Portes 1987; Bendick and Egan 1986). But only five business owners in this study had prior business experience. Two factors helped overcome this. Twelve entrepreneurs described a family member or friend in their country of origin who served as a role model, suggesting the influence of class factors. Second, more than half the business owners in this study had another career before they went into business. This pattern seemed particularly striking among the more successful Puerto Rican business owners, many of whom rose through the ranks of city government. In the absence of a fully developed Latino institutional network, public and private sector agencies provided them with the social contacts, skills, and access to resources that other groups, such as Cubans glean from their own ethnic institutions (Portes and Manning 1986). For example, two men parlayed a one-hour Spanish radio program they began with War on Poverty program funding into control over a large share of the Latino communications market. They are currently trying to purchase the only twenty-four-hour Spanish-speaking radio station in New England.

Coethnics provide critical technical assistance and skills training largely free of charge. Most store owners reportedly learned their skills through on-the-job training in Latino-owned stores or from friends and family members who helped them informally as they went along. Only five business owners sought formal training or credentials. Some believed that additional training would be valuable but felt they could not stop working to go to school. Others claimed that "you don't need training to get into business. You learn. You look for people to help you with what you don't know."

For these business owners, social relations are not limited to a particular realm; economic structures overlap with kinship, political, religious, and social ones. One's father or uncle may also be one's employer, banker, and confidant. One uses these social relationships, as opposed to bureaucratic or institutional channels, to resolve problems (Fitzpatrick 1987). "When they first arrive, Dominicans have to go through a year of transition. They have to adapt to the system of cleaning the street, the system of having to pay one's taxes. . . . At home, they are used to a system in which you ignore your ticket because you can resolve it through a friend. They are used to a system of friends working it out" (Clothing store owner). Furthermore, just as social relationships are not compartmentalized, the notion of time and the rules guiding business owners are also fluid and porous. Rules are necessary, but some amount of rule breaking is expected and condoned. Several store owners reported that they often acted in ways they thought of as telling "little white lies." They described an implicit hierarchy of rules, some more malleable than others. For example, allowing illegal gambling in the back room of one's store is acceptable but drug dealing is not. Some rules, one owner said, are "only meant for the big guys. They do not apply to small store owners like me."

Labor

Family members or friends worked in approximately two-thirds of the businesses in the study; about one-half were paid whereas the others received gifts or on-the-job training in exchange for their time. Business owners claimed that hiring family members improves business performance because (1) it lowers costs; (2) they have more *confianza* (trust) in family members, particularly with respect to money; (3) they can depend on family members to change their work hours or work extended hours at short notice; and (4) they can establish more egalitarian relationships with their employees, making them more comfortable with their role as boss and heightening productivity.

Ethnic Consumers

Approximately one-third of the stores in the study sold ethnic products. Another third sold products that were ethnic by virtue of style, such as children's clothing or furniture that appealed to a particularly Latino aesthetic. The remaining group sold generic services like hair cutting, travel arrangements, or income tax preparation that were ethnic by virtue of the milieu in which they were exchanged. A botanica owner, who sold taboo religious articles for Santero and Espiritista ceremonies, also sold gift items, greeting cards, party favors, and music. She explained that she needed to give customers a legitimate reason for entering her store because she sold "forbidden" goods.

Eighty percent of the business owners reported that from 60 to 99 percent of their customers are Latino. Whereas prior research found that other immigrant groups, such as Asians, Hindustanis, and Turks, preferred to sell to other ethnic groups because their coethnics were allegedly cheap and tried to cheat them, Latino business owners seemed pleased to deal with their compatriots (Waldinger, Aldrich and Ward 1990). Business owners know the majority of their clients personally, either from community life in Boston or from their country of origin. Several respondents mentioned the tendency among Dominicans to frequent stores owned by people from their hometowns. A tailor shop owner, who is not from Bani but whose shop is located in an overwhelmingly Banilejo neighborhood, coped with this problem by hiring a tailor from that city. Many customers come to his store because they used this same tailor in the Dominican Republic.

Ethnic Salesmanship

Store owners earn a reputation for the quality of their merchandise or the way they treat their customers, which allegedly spreads by word-of-mouth across the state. They attract clients based on this reputation and their visibility in the Latino community. A clothing store owner realized that his success depended too much on personal relationships with clients after sales plummeted when he assumed a less public role in his store.

Store owners are public figures whose face-to-face interactions have repercussions extending far beyond their store walls. Alienating one customer can have a serious multiplier effect as this bridal shop owner explained, "It is worse to have one unhappy customer than fifty happy ones because the unhappy customer can talk to fifty more customers that are around that are planning to come into the place and say don't go there because it is not worth it." Business owners also evaluate clients based on their reputation within the community. If a new client comes recommended by friends and family they are deemed reliable. For example, "If a person recommends their cousin or their neighbor, they say this person will pay you, if they don't pay you, I will pay you. It is like credit. The clients know that if a person recommends them, they feel pressure to pay because of their reputation. This continues growing and later there are two people to put on the pressure; the person who sold you the merchandise [and] the person who recommended you" (Gift store owner).

An implicit set of norms and values govern the economic exchanges that take place between salesperson and customer. This shared world-view changes the nature of salesmanship. The shopkeeper and client are closer because they "are of the same blood, of the same culture." Instead of the anonymous, impersonal relationship many Anglos have with store proprietors, the Latino customer expects to know the shop owner well. In response, shopkeepers try to make their customers feel as if they just came over for a chat. Most take the approach exemplified by the restaurant owner who unknowingly thought up the title for this paper when he reported greeting all his customers as *primo* (cousin) to make them feel as if they are part of his family and welcome in his home.

This highly personalized, customer-specific sales strategy, which respondents call *buen trato* (good treatment) includes keeping track of customers' style or color preferences, inquiring about their health problems, and remembering when they have not been into the store for a long time. As one clothing store owner explained, "The client, you have to get to know him. At least with my clients, I know almost all of them by name. I keep a card file with the names of their children. . . . Clients like to be treated with familiarity. When they haven't come for a while, you say where have you been, were you sick? Most clients come regularly, at least two times a month."

A grocery store owner described his customer relations: "Once a Hispanic person starts going to a Hispanic store he becomes your friend for as long as you have that store. If you go to a 'Lil Peach or one of those stores, you see the same guy everyday. He tells you 'hi' and that is it. You can't establish a conversation with him. Over here, we know the history of most of our customers. The problems that they have. We get invited to all the weddings around. We get invited to the baptisms." Because many stores sell similar products to the same potential client pool, yet most reported facing little competition, *buen trato* seems to function as the product differentiation mechanism used to choose one store over the other.

Customer and store owners seem to feel a sense of obligation and involvement with each other that extends beyond the purely economic. Rational action involves taking these social considerations into account because every economic act has social consequences that directly affect the relationship between buyer and seller and between the seller and the rest of the group. When the store owner pays attention to the customer, the customer often feels impelled to buy something, as this record store owner described: "Morally, you feel an obligation. If you are treated well, you feel bad saying no. . . . If you let someone speak for three hours, it's likely that you don't have the nerve to say I won't buy anything."

Bodega owners in the Spanish-speaking Caribbean often give credit during the dead season when no work is available. In Boston, extending credit is also an integral, expected component of the economic exchange. Most store owners reported selling at least some merchandise on credit; some sold on credit to as many as 15 percent of their customers. Store owners used credit granting as a way to demonstrate that they had trust (*confianza*) in their clients. "My customers have an established routine. They come in to buy something on Wednesday even though they have to buy it on credit and they know they will get paid on Friday and they can pay me then. If I do not give them credit, they will feel insulted. I am showing that I have put my trust in them, that I have the trust in them to give them something without anything in return. Then other clients speak well about me to other clients. I have to protect my reputation. If I don't give credit, I will lose customers" (Clothing store owner).

Tenants felt a strong sense of obligation to pay their coethnic landlords, and creditees felt they must repay their debts to maintain their status within the community. "One thing I learned at Mission Hill Variety. I am more successful giving credit to Hispanics than Americans. Americans fail. They don't pay you. I learned that through the years. They never come back. . . . I don't have that problem with Hispanics. It is a more personal relationship. They feel that they have to pay you to maintain their honor. Because when they see you on the street they will die" (Large grocery store owner). Extending credit is a particularly interesting example of the way in which economic rationality is socially constructed. Many community development practitioners view giving credit as bad business practice—they believe that credit strains a business' cash flow and that debts often go unpaid. In contrast, Latino business owners who opt to discontinue credit risk alienating their customer base. Indeed, it may be good business to continue granting credit because the customers' desire to maintain their reputation in the community encourages high repayment rates. Among Dominicans, the practice of bargaining over price is also common. Because owners understand that customers will expect discounts and that the community at large will find out if they do not lower their prices, they normally raise the initial asking price above what they expect to receive. "You say twenty dollars and they offer you fifteen dollars. They always want a lower price even if you are selling on credit. I tell them when you go to Filene's or Jordan Marsh, you can't ask for a discount. They tell me that is why [they] don't shop there" (Clothing store owner).

Finally, owners sometimes charge customers according to what they think a particular client can pay. For example, a men's clothing store owner does not put price tags on his merchandise. He charges based on what he knows about a particular customer's financial status or, if he does not know clients personally, his subjective assessment of their purchasing power. There was only one entrepreneur who was known for overcharging his customers. Ironically, this is the most successful business owner in the study, who no longer depends on Latino customers for his livelihood. Because most store owners still do, a system of internal cost controls is at work—a store owner cannot afford to earn a reputation for overcharging his customers or many clients will stop patronizing his store.

In sum, social resources generate much of the capital, labor, and expertise that drive these businesses. They allow a small group of potential entrepreneurs to overcome the barriers to entry raised by their lack of experience, skills, and the opportunity structure. In general, the resulting businesses are moderately successful, low-growth enterprises that are well suited for this insular ethnic milieu.

If business owners want to expand or move into the non-ethnic market, however, they need access to resources and skills outside the community. The same resources that enable business owners to develop these small businesses may create inherent constraints to business performance. In approximately two-thirds of the businesses in this study, there was apparently a threshold beyond which ethnic resources, in fact, impeded further growth. For example, because most business owners do not work with banks, their ability to expand, take risks, or withstand slow periods is largely contingent on the size and liquidity of the community's coffers. Many entrepreneurs pay cash for their merchandise; therefore, they do not establish credit worthiness with suppliers and are restricted as to the amount of inventory they can purchase at any given time.

The fact that Boston's Latino small business sector is primarily con-

133

fined to the retail and service sectors also constrains business development because owners only have access to the information, skills, and
techniques that flow within this fairly small, homogeneous network.
Few new ideas, innovations, or information about non-ethnic business
opportunities seem to infiltrate the community. Business owners are
just beginning to form the types of trade and professional organizations
that have strengthened and expanded business networks among other
foreign-born groups. In addition, because most businesses continue
to sell ethnic products to a largely Hispanic clientele they still face a
bounded market with limited purchasing power. Finally, for fear of alienating or offending their customers, business owners must continue to
grant credit, bargain about prices, or employ family members even in
those cases where the economic costs of such practices seem to out-
weigh their benefits.

Small business ownership, then, is not a viable mobility strategy for
most Latinos. The opportunity structure impedes business development. Most community members lack the capital and skills needed
to mount successful businesses. And those individuals who do go into
business confront internal constraints to performance. Such a view,
however, does not take sufficient note of the critical social role these
businesses play in providing for the Latino community and the way
business owners themselves assess their own success. I focus on these
issues in the rest of the chapter.

The Social Role of Latino Businesses

In the early days of the Puerto Rican community, small businesses dou-
bled as impromptu social centers where people came to exchange news,
gossip, or simply pass time together. This is still true today. Immigrants
bring this practice with them from home, where the bodega is often the
village gathering place. In Boston, the barbershop is full, not because
everyone is getting a haircut, but because people socialize in commercial spaces rather than their homes. This even happens in large stores:
"That customer is here every morning. He is here all day. That is typical
of a Puerto Rican store. . . . The employees even like to come and talk to
us on their days off. The store is like another room in their house" (Large
grocery store owner).

Customers often come to stores just to greet the store owners even if they do not need anything. "People who come frequently, it is like a social visit. Sometimes people come and they say, oh, I came only to say hello. They tell their problems and ask advice. They ask for help and emotional support" (Record store owner). Store owners generally felt it was their job to help their customers and that it contributed to their success, often stating, "It is the role of the businessperson to give back a little of what they have received from the community." A botanica owner described her job as part social worker. A large grocery store owner reported that "I am an important figure in this community because I am supplying families with food." The fact that he has never been robbed, even though his store is in a high-crime area, is proof to him that others see him as fulfilling his responsibility to the collective good.

Business owners also frequently contribute or loan money. "If anybody dies in this community, the first place they come is over here. It is like in Puerto Rico, they come over here, we pick out a big can, we make a collection. We start first with all our employees and sometimes we collect up to five hundred dollars for any burial in the community for anybody that dies. If you go to any American store, you can't tell them to do that. They won't do that. This store is like a community institution" (Large grocery store owner). The role of the store owner as money lender is especially important because there are few, if any, bank branches in Latino neighborhoods. Store owners represent a rapid, no-questions-asked source of funds for people who would probably not qualify for bank loans, though some owners charge higher-than-average interest rates. Many store owners offer check-cashing services.

Store owners also create an informal social service system that complements or often substitutes for the formal one. For example, they sell products to those who do not have enough money or the means to travel to large chains and malls. They ease the terms of exchange by allowing people to buy small quantities, such as a single piece of cake or half a loaf of bread, and by granting people credit. And store owners often allow people to take their purchases even if they are a few dollars short.

In essence, store owners in Boston play a comparable social role to businesses in their communities of origin. They are the provider-of-last-resort when people need food or money—the ethnic version of a social safety net. They help community members find jobs, housing, and health care. They are role models, therapists, and teachers. The community conducts its social life and affirms its identity within the walls of their stores. Particularly important is their practice of selling items on credit, in small quantities, and at the local level, so that a supply of goods to the very poor is ensured.

Images of Success

One might assume that most entrepreneurs would be frustrated when faced with the prospect of limited growth. In the United States, we tend to equate bigger with better and value only those things that have the potential to expand (Lasch 1991). Latino business owners seem to be guided by a different notion of success. In general, their goal is to run their businesses so that their economic needs are satisfied but they are still able to follow the community's social rules and fulfill their social responsibilities. A strong desire for autonomy and independence, as well as economic advancement, motivated most of the entrepreneurs in this study to go into business. They typically explained, "My ambition was to have my own business so I wouldn't have to work for anybody. I didn't dream of having a lot of money." Few business owners defined success in monetary terms. Most often, they described it like these business owners:

> I don't measure success moneywise, I measure success on personal accomplishment, friendship, what kind of people are you surrounded with, who can you call in case anything happens, how has your family been raised. How many of your children have been educated properly, how many have been in jail, how many have been abusing the system, how many are not law abiding citizens? I measure achievement in that way (Record store owner).

> As I know a lot of people and everyone has come to me, I always give them a hand. . . . I know that people come to the store because at some time, I helped them with something: social security, marital problems, welfare. . . . This is my success. My business has been able to shine because people have seen me with good eyes. They haven't been able to say look at that one who robs, he never worried about us. (Clothing store owner)

Most business owners expressed modest ambitions. They generally wanted to live comfortably, with some degree of security, and be able to educate their children: "There are people who get pleasure out of seeing a packet of money. I get pleasure out of watching my children enjoy what that money can buy. . . . I personally don't aspire to have a big bank account. I want to be able to educate my children day to day. I aspire to be able to go to sleep knowing that if they get sick, there will be health for them" (Restaurant owner). Owners claimed that their lifestyles would not change even if they became wealthy: "If I am meant to be a millionaire then it is meant to be, but it won't change me socially. I'll still eat Latino, go to Latino dances, live among Latinos" (Radio station owner).

Several factors may explain Latino business owners' aspirations and ideals. First, both the Dominican Republic and Puerto Rico are generally characterized as deeply stratified societies. Business owners' visions of their possibilities for social mobility are framed by their experiences in their home country—societies in which life as an escalator is not a prospect for everyone. Second, in societies in which social status is ascribed at birth, individuals tend to be judged by their personal qualities and behavior rather than their ability to accumulate wealth. Thus, material accumulation, as a goal in itself, assumes less importance. Third, twenty-two business owners stated that they had little if any ongoing, social contacts with Anglos. Most lived and socialized almost entirely among Latinos. The reference group against which they measured their success was the Latino community in Boston and at home. Relative to their compatriots here and in their countries of origin, most business owners enjoyed greater financial success and occupational status. In the same vein, business owners who progress too far ahead of their peers run the risk of alienating the only community they belong to. Since business owners' social lives take place almost entirely within the Latino community, they may constrain their behavior so as not to get too far ahead of the rest of the group. The fact that so many business owners continue living in the same community, even after they can afford to move out, attests to this. As one respondent put it, "The goal is to make the ghetto better rather than to move out of the ghetto."

What becomes clear from talking with Latino business owners is that they are not simply motivated by profit maximization—they also try to achieve approval, status, and power within the community. The economic act is not merely an exchange of goods—it is also an exchange of respect and trust. These practices make such businesses work.

Conclusions and Policy Implications

Latino business owners' experiences lend credence to Granovetter's notion (1985) of economic embeddedness. They are not rational self-interested actors who are minimally effected by social relations, nor have they internalized normative standards so deeply that the social relations surrounding them have little impact on their behavior. Instead, Latino entrepreneurs are "deeply embedded in concrete ongoing systems of social relations in which culture is continuously constructed and reconstructed" (Granovetter 1985). The embeddedness of their economic activities within their community generates essential tools with which they conduct business.

This study points out some ways in which the same dense grid of social expectations and reciprocal obligations that engenders and sustains Latino businesses also constrains them. But despite their low-growth potential and limited economic returns, these businesses are successful. To think otherwise is to deify progress and to ignore the implicit rationality of forging, testing, and servicing social relationships, though this may inhibit economic performance. It is precisely those practices that allow Latino businesses to function at the level they do. Moreover, a different vision of achievement, more consistent with stability rather than unchecked accumulation and growth, appears to drive the business owners in this study. In general they feel successful and express satisfaction with their achievements.

Future research should look more closely at the differences among Latino groups. A larger, more longitudinal study will most certainly reveal differences in the business strategies employed by national and religious subgroups. A more comparative approach that included native-born ethnics and non-ethnics would also help to clarify the extent to which ethnic entrepreneurship, as described here, is also practiced by business owners in small towns and other tightly knit urban villages. It would also be useful to look at the role of the informal sector in Latino small business development.

Notes

1. Business participation rate = number of self-employed multiplied by 1,000 divided by total persons in group (Waldinger, Aldrich, and Ward 1990).

2. This study was partially funded by the Mauricio Gastón Institute for Latino Community Development and Public Policy at the University of Massachusetts.

3. These districts include Egleston Square in Jamaica Plain, Centre Street in Jamaica Plain, Dudley Street in Roxbury, Bowdoin / Geneva Avenues in Dorchester, the South End, and East Cambridge.

4. For the purposes of this study, I use Stinchcombe's definition of the petit bourgeois labor market: wholesale trade, retail trade, taxicab services, real estate, detective and protective services, personal services, sports, entertainment, and

recreation (Stinchcombe 1979). I did not include professionals such as doctors and lawyers who are also self-employed.

5. Service firms are defined as personal, business, repair, health, legal, educational, and recreational services.

References

Bendick, Marc, and Mary Lou Egan. 1986. "Self Employment Initiatives in the U.S.: Lessons for National Policy." Paper prepared for the Ford Foundation.

Boston Redevelopment Authority. 1987. "Results of the 1985 Household Survey." Vol. 3, Labor Force. June.

Fitzpatrick, Joseph P. 1987. *Puerto Rican Americans: The Meaning of Migration to the Mainland.* Englewood Cliffs, N.J.: Prentice Hall.

Fratoe, Frank A., and Ronald L. Meeks. 1985. "Business Participation Rates of the 50 Largest U.S. Ancestry Groups: Preliminary Report." U.S. Department of Commerce, Minority Business Development Agency.

Georges, Eugenia. 1990. *The Making of a Transnational Community.* New York: Columbia University Press.

Granovetter, Mark. 1985. "Economic Action and Social Structure: The Problem of Embeddedness." *American Journal of Sociology* 91.

Harrison, Bennett. 1988. "The Economic Development of Massachusetts." In *The Massachusetts Miracle: High Technology and Economic Revitalization,* edited by David Lampe. Cambridge: MIT Press.

Lasch, Christopher. 1991. *The True and Only Heaven.* New York: Norton.

Levine, Melvin F. 1991. "Opportunities for Retail Stores in Boston's Neighborhoods." Monograph prepared for the Boston Redevelopment Authority.

Light, Ivan, and Edna Bonacich. 1988. *Immigrant Entrepreneurs.* Berkeley: University of California Press.

Massachusetts Commission against Discrimination. 1991. "Public Hearings on M/WBEs: Report, Findings, and Recommendations," March.

Melendez, Edwin. 1994. "Latino Poverty and Economic Development." In *Latino Poverty and Economic Development in Massachusetts,* edited by Edwin Melendez and Mirren Uriarte. Boston: University of Massachusetts Press.

Osterman, Paul. 1990. "In the Midst of Plenty: A Profile of Boston and Its Poor." Boston: Boston Foundation.

Pedraza-Bailey, Silvia, and Roger Waldinger. 1991. "Ethnic Enterprise: Self-Employment among Hispanic and Asian Immigrants in Chicago." Research proposal to the National Science Foundation.

Piore, Michael J. 1979. *Birds of Passage.* Cambridge: Cambridge University Press.

Portes, Alejandro. 1987. "The Social Origins of the Cuban Enclave Economy in Miami." *Sociological Perspectives* 30.

Portes, Alejandro, and Robert Manning. 1986. "The Immigrant Enclave: Theory and Empirical Examples." In *Competitive Ethnic Relations,* edited by Susan Olzak and Joanne Nagel. Orlando, Fl.: Academic Press.

Stinchcombe, Arthur L. 1979. "Social Mobility in Industrial Labor Markets." *Acta Sociologica* 22.

U.S. Department of Commerce. 1971a. Bureau of the Census. *Census of Population, 1970.* Washington, D.C.: U.S. Government Printing Office.

——. Bureau of the Census. 1971b. *Survey of Minority-Owned Business Enterprises, 1969.* Washington, D.C.: U.S. Government Printing Office.

——. Bureau of the Census. 1974. *Survey of Minority-Owned Business Enterprises, 1972.* Washington, D.C.: U.S. Government Printing Office.

——. Bureau of the Census. 1979. *Survey of Minority-Owned Business Enterprises, 1977.* Washington, D.C.: U.S. Government Printing Office.

——. Bureau of the Census. 1982. *Census of Population, 1980.* Washington, D.C.: U.S. Government Printing Office.

——. Bureau of the Census. 1985. *Survey of Minority-Owned Business Enterprises, 1982.* Washington, D.C.: U.S. Government Printing Office.

——. Bureau of the Census. 1990. *Survey of Minority-Owned Business Enterprises, 1987.* Washington, D.C.: U.S. Government Printing Office.

——. Bureau of the Census. 1992. *Census of Population, 1990.* Washington, D.C.: U.S. Government Printing Office.

Waldinger, Roger, Howard E. Aldrich, and Robin Ward. 1990. *Ethnic Entrepreneurs.* Newbury Park, Calif.: Sage.

Chapter 7

The Culture
of Entrepreneurship
among Khmer Refugees

Nancy J. Smith-Hefner

Studies of Southeast Asian economies consistently emphasize the pivotal role of ethnic Chinese in business and entrepreneurship. In Cambodia, as in neighboring Vietnam and, to a lesser degree, Laos, ethnic Chinese controlled the largest portion of the economy before the disruption of the American war in Indochina (Willmott 1967; Whitmore 1985). Immigrating under forced conditions to the United States, Sino-Khmer have continued to play a primary role in economic activity among Khmer refugees. Within the metropolitan Boston Khmer community, Sino-Khmer make up only about 6 percent of the total Khmer population, but they account for an estimated 85 percent of business activity. By contrast, among pure Khmer (*khmae sot*) the incidence of entrepreneurship is extremely low, even lower than that among neighboring non-Chinese Southeast Asian populations like the Vietnamese.[1]

As members of the most recent wave of Southeast Asian immigration, the Khmer in metropolitan Boston have faced a number of structural obstacles to entrepreneurial activity. Most notable among these obstacles are their lack of capital, low levels of education, and limited English proficiency. Unlike economic immigrants to the United States, who typically come prepared to sacrifice and take risks to underwrite business success, most Khmer refugees left their country reluctantly, under the extreme duress of the war and Pol Pot holocaust. A large proportion of them came from rural rather than urban backgrounds. They often arrived in the United States, therefore, with few of the capital or social resources necessary for business enterprise, and ill-prepared for the challenge of adapting to a new way of life.[2]

Structural influences, however, have not been the only ones shaping the limited involvement of Khmer in business enterprise. Rather than investing in privately owned business enterprises, for example, Khmer refugees here have tended to place what resources they do command in initiatives related to the reconstitution of social community and to their own standing within it. These and other sociocultural influences serve to channel economic resources into status and social relations rather than more individualistic enterprises. In committing their social and economic resources in this fashion, Khmer refugees have ceded the entrepreneurial ground to their Sino-Khmer colleagues, inadvertently reproducing what has long been a critical cultural marker distinguishing ordinary Khmer from Sino-Khmer.

Based on ethnographic research within the Greater Metropolitan Boston Khmer community, this chapter examines patterns of entrepreneurship among Khmer refugees and considers the sociocultural factors that support the continued prominence of Sino-Khmer in Khmer entrepreneurial activities. Research for this chapter included thirty-five in-depth interviews with Khmer small business owners and entrepreneurs conducted during an eight-month period from February to September 1991. These interviews were supplemented with information from some seventy-five interviews with members of the Khmer community who were not directly involved in business activities, collected in the preceding eighteen months.[3] The study was generously supported by the Institute for the Study of Economic Culture at Boston University. It constitutes a segment of a larger research project concerning the social and cultural adaptation of Khmer refugees to life in the United States.

The Khmer Community in Metropolitan Boston

The Boston area has a sizable population of Khmer refugees. Though recent numbers have diminished somewhat because of the economic downturn in the Northeast that began in the late 1980s, today there are at least twenty thousand Khmer living in Boston and the surrounding area. Community leaders estimate that there are three thousand Khmer in Revere; eighteen hundred in Lynn; fifteen hundred in Chelsea and six hundred in East Boston. Another one thousand or so Khmer are scattered throughout Allston, Brighton, and Quincy. In addition, as many as twelve thousand to fourteen thousand Khmer live in the city of Lowell, one hour north of Boston, giving the Lowell community the largest concentration of Khmer in the United States after Long Beach, California.[4]

Most Boston-area Khmer arrived in the early to mid-1980s as part of the third and most recent wave of Southeast Asian immigration to the United States (Ebihara 1985). Many are actually secondary migrants who came to eastern Massachusetts after having first been settled in other states. They were drawn to the area by the reports from friends and relatives of less expensive housing, more generous social programs, and employment in local seafood factories, medical laboratories, and electronics companies (Vlahou 1988; Costello 1989). They also came to eastern Massachusetts in search of a large and integral Khmer community.

Khmer tend to live in clusters in low-income neighborhoods among other immigrants, or minorities, or both. In these neighborhoods it is not unusual to find the local Hispanic store selling a few Asian household goods, condiments, and large sacks of imported Thai rice. Those Khmer who live within easy access of Boston's Chinatown rely on stores there to fill their ethnic, social, and business needs.[5] Khmer also frequent Vietnamese stores, which are more numerous then Khmer establishments. In the cities of Revere and Lowell, however, significant clusters of Khmer stores and businesses cater to the Khmer population and, to a much smaller degree, non-Khmer locals as well. Khmer say they prefer to shop in Cambodian stores; those who live at a distance may drive into Revere or Lowell on the weekend to stock up on ethnic goods, conduct their business, visit friends, and eat a bowl of *slaa mcuu* (sour soup) at a favorite restaurant.

In contrast to earlier waves of Southeast Asian immigration to the United States, which included significant numbers of elite urbanites, members of the third wave of immigration tend to be more rural, less well-educated, and, correspondingly, less proficient in English (Ebihara 1985). As members of this most recent wave of immigration, the great majority of Boston-area Khmer came from the Cambodian countryside. Most worked as farmers cultivating rice or fruits and vegetables and had only limited experience with urban life before their arrival in the United States. The majority of these individuals also had relatively little formal education. Most did not complete elementary education in Cambodia; many, including the majority of women, had considerably less (Smith-Hefner 1990).

Under the Pol Pot regime of Democratic Kampuchea (1975–79), the Khmer Rouge directed their harshest initiatives at the educated and urban segments of the population, a significant percentage of whom perished (Vickery 1984; Hood & Ablin 1987). Of the surviving Khmer middle class, most have settled in California and Washington, D.C., joining other members of the Khmer and Southeast Asian elite. The few middle-class or elite Khmer who have moved to the Boston area tend to distance themselves from the main centers of urban settlement by moving out of urban areas into outlying suburbs where housing is affordable, schools are of higher quality, and there is, as a result, much less opportunity for interaction in the refugee community.

Rates of welfare dependency for Cambodians in the Boston area, as reported among Khmer refugees more generally, are close to 50 percent (Boston Persistent Poverty Project 1992). Figures on poverty rates for Boston-area Khmer, as distinct from other Asian groups, are not available. But it has been estimated that, because of the low level of support provided by welfare and refugee cash assistance, 64 percent of those Southeast Asians who rely on these services live below the poverty line (Caplan, Whitmore, & Bui 1985, 189, cited in Gold 1994). Entrepreneurship is one possible avenue for refugees attempting to move out of the cycle of poverty and welfare dependency. However, although some Khmer—particularly Sino-Khmer—have become successful independent businesspeople, small business employment has locked others into low-paying, labor intensive, menial jobs without health insurance or other benefits.

The Sino-Khmer Community

For several reasons, determining the precise number of Chinese, or Sino-Khmer, in the U.S. Khmer refugee community is difficult. Government statistics typically do not distinguish between majority and minority ethnic groups in the Southeast Asian population, providing no figures on Sino-Khmer.[6] The issue is further complicated because Khmer themselves do not agree on the criteria for distinguishing Sino-Khmer from ordinary Khmer, in large part because, unlike the ethnic pattern seen in some Southeast Asian countries, the boundary between pure Khmer and Sino-Khmer in Cambodia has itself long been quite diffuse (Willmott 1967).

Relations between the majority population and Chinese minority in prewar Cambodia were notably less antagonistic than in other countries of Southeast Asia (Willmott 1967; Purcell 1973). Under the French colonial government, Khmer and Chinese alike suffered from discriminatory measures that favored Vietnamese over the local population. Moreover, Chinese in Cambodia were far from their homeland, and many lost contact with aspects of Chinese ethnicity. This was especially true of Chinese who lived in rural areas of Cambodia where intermarriage with local Khmer was quite common. In contrast to their situation in neighboring Southeast Asian countries, approximately 40 percent of the Chinese in Cambodia lived in the countryside. Few of these were rice farmers, however, as were most rural Khmer. These rural Chinese worked instead as small merchants, market gardeners, or rice traders (Willmott 1967, 42–48). Many of them were eventually assimilated into Khmer culture and society.

Khmer commonly say that a person is Chinese if she or he is one-quarter Chinese, that is, has at least one Chinese grandparent. But this simple measure is complicated by the fact that the likelihood of being Chinese is greater where the ancestry continues to be traced through males rather than females, preserving the patrilineal descent favored by Chinese. (Khmer kinship is cognatic not patrilineal.) A Chinese woman who marries a Khmer man is less likely to see her children or grandchildren remain Chinese than is a man. The decisive variable in determining Chineseness, however, lies less in ancestry or descent alone than in a broader array of social practices that serve as indices of Chinese identity. These include whether one celebrates the Chinese New Year or Moon Festival, whether one maintains a small ancestral shrine in one's home or business, and, perhaps most important, whether one still speaks or at least understands a dialect of Chinese.

Community leaders in metropolitan Boston estimate that 3 percent of the area's refugees are Sino-Khmer from a relatively pure, easily identifiable Chinese background (*cau chen*). By contrast, because of the high degree of intermarriage among Khmer and Chinese and the porousness of the ethnic boundary, the percentage of people identifying themselves as Sino-Khmer (*khmae chen*), whether partially or predominantly Chinese, is between 6 and 10 percent of the population.[7] I use the figure of 6 percent here and include within it both those considered pure Chinese, or Khmer Chinese, and those who are Sino-Khmer—who have at least one-quarter Chinese ancestry and who also maintain at least some Chinese cultural practices. Using this population as the baseline, it appears that at least 85 percent of Khmer business enterprises in the Boston area are run by members of this group, which I refer to simply as Sino-Khmer. This figure is based on the estimates of community leaders and is consistent with the results of my interviews among Khmer entrepreneurs.

The predominance of Sino-Khmer in Cambodian business activity is readily apparent in all the major centers of refugee settlement in metropolitan Boston. In the community of Revere, just north of the city of Boston, for example, one finds the largest concentration of Khmer business enterprise in the metropolitan area. In a run-down, congested, two-block region just outside of Revere's main business district are five groceries, two jewelry stores, one photo store, three video stores, three restaurants, and one beauty parlor, all owned by Cambodian entrepreneurs. Four of the five groceries, both of the jewelry stores, one of the video stores, the photo store, and all three of the restaurants are owned by Cambodians of Chinese ancestry. Moreover, the non-Chinese businesses tend to be smaller and less capital intensive than their Sino-Khmer counterparts, with notably smaller stocks and significantly smaller patronage.

The same pattern of Sino-Khmer dominance in small business is equally visible in what is perhaps the most impressive center of Khmer enterprise in Massachusetts, located in a small but pleasantly modern mall in the city of Lowell. The mall itself was built by a Sino-Khmer businessman using a loan secured from a U.S. bank. Sino-Khmer operate almost all of the mall's businesses. These include a video store, an insurance company, a paralegal service, a beauty salon, a jewelry store, a restaurant, a laundromat, and a dentist's office (operated by an American-trained Taiwanese dentist assisted by his Sino-Khmer wife). The only business in the complex not owned by a Sino-Khmer is a small clothing store.

The Economic Role of the Chinese in Cambodia

These examples raise the obvious question of how to explain Sino-Khmer economic domination within the refugee community. In part, that role can be traced to the historical predominance of Sino-Khmer in the Cambodian economy. During the colonial period, the French adopted a number of policies that discouraged the development of a well-educated, entrepreneurial, and politically sophisticated Khmer middle class. For the most part, they viewed the Cambodian people as "indolent peasants who did not have the necessary aptitudes for education or technical skills" (Willmott 1967, 34). As a result, they preferred to train and employ Vietnamese as political administrators in the country, which they considered a primitive backwater compared to the more "civilized" culture of Vietnam. Similarly, in economic affairs, the French (like the Dutch in the East Indies) preferred to utilize Chinese as middlemen in trade and enterprise (Purcell 1973; Bonacich 1973). Although colonial reports reveal a high degree of distrust on the part of the French for the Chinese, the French are said to have admired Chinese economic skills—at least as long as those skills were not exercised in large-scale and estate enterprises, where the French sought to exercise a monopoly. Chinese were able to supply goods to the colonial government at much lower prices than French companies could. They also proved skilled at selling imported goods and collecting produce and taxes from the countryside (Willmott 1967, 47).

When the French left Cambodia, the Khmer expelled the Vietnamese from administrative positions within the government, securing a prestigious array of bureaucratic positions for native Khmer. Khmer were unable to act as boldly with Chinese businesses, however, because so much of the economy depended upon Sino-Khmer. Expropriation of Chinese business was also rendered unattractive by virtue of the fact that the government benefited from a special tax levied on foreign, that is, Chinese, business activity. In 1956, in an effort to limit Chinese economic influence, the government barred Chinese from some eighteen types of enterprise. These included rice trading, shipping, salt, second-hand dealing, and loans (Whitmore 1985, 65; Willmott 1967, 45–46). Many Chinese were able to circumvent these regulations, however, by registering their businesses in the names of their Cambodian wives or other Khmer relatives. Sino-Khmer thus maintained their dominant role in the Cambodian economy. In the late 1960s, the anthropologist William E. Willmott (1967, 64) estimated that the Chinese accounted for some 90 percent of the population engaged in commerce in Cambodia and some 95 percent of the merchant class itself.

This same pattern of Chinese predominance is being reproduced in the Khmer community in the United States. Whatever the precise nature of the Chinese economic advantage, prior business experience seems to be one element that ensures Chinese competitiveness. Almost all the Sino-Khmer business owners in the metropolitan Boston community were either business owners in Cambodia, or came from business families.

Chinese Identity and Cultural Values

The generally high degree of assimilation and the relative lack of animosity toward the Chinese on the part of the Khmer complicate the task of identifying Chinese cultural values that might influence economic patterns. Moreover, as a result of intermarriage, Sino-Khmer often do not seem different in appearance or behavior from ordinary Khmer. Although Cambodians themselves say they can tell the difference, the lightness of skin that is typically remarked upon is not always a reliable indicator of ethnic identity. There is, nonetheless, an assumption of difference. As one young Sino-Khmer male explained, "Among Cambodians, we can tell who is Chinese from 'the look.' And like, if we see two guys walking down the street and one is Chinese Cambodian and one is pure Cambodian . . . and let's say both of them are very poor, they have no money in their pockets, Cambodians will think that the Chinese guy has $500 in his pocket. That's the way we all think. It's the quality of the look."

Nor are family names (*sae chen*) a particularly reliable indicator of Chinese ethnicity. Although family name and, more generally, clan associations have played an important role in facilitating economic activity among Chinese in other overseas communities,[8] they are apparently not operative among Sino-Khmer in the United States. In fact, the only association Chinese Khmer admit to belonging to, and then only in a very loose sense, are Chinese language groups.

There are five major Chinese language (or dialect) groups represented in Cambodia (Willmott 1967, 17). The majority of the Sino-Khmer I interviewed in the Boston area community are Teochieu speakers, although a few have intermarried with Hokkien or Cantonese speakers. This accords with Willmott's figures that three out of every four Chinese in Cambodia are Teochieu speaking and that Teochieu make up nine out of ten rural Chinese (Willmott 1967, 17).

Whatever their home language, if circumstances allowed, most Sino-Khmer children in Cambodia, especially males, were sent by their parents to Chinese school to study Mandarin for at least a short time. Even in the United States, some Sino-Khmer children attend weekend Mandarin school. Perhaps not surprisingly, regional language identity and, to a somewhat lesser extent, the preservation of Chinese (that is, Mandarin) language capabilities through schooling are viewed by both Sino-Khmer and ordinary Khmer as important indices of Chinese identity.

At the same time, many adult Chinese regard their previous attendance at Chinese schools in Cambodia as a strategy adopted by their parents in the face of obstacles to full Sino-Khmer participation in Cambodian society. Sino-Khmer, for example, were routinely excluded from government jobs, and at various times in recent history the government sought to bar them from other kinds of employment. One middle-aged Chinese male explained, "In Cambodia, you have to go to a public school to get a government job. But even for [ordinary] Cambodians maybe only 10 percent of the graduates from the state schools can get a government job and the rest have to become farmers or to do some other job. Chinese parents are practical. They know that if they send their kids to Chinese school they will be good in math and in business. So better for them to go to the Chinese school. Because if you know the Chinese language it's easy to get a job." Chinese parents were aware that government employment could be secured only through public education. But they also knew that their children were at a disadvantage in competing with ordinary Cambodian children in the public schools, with their strong emphasis on Khmer language and culture. Although Sino-Khmer children learned spoken Khmer fairly quickly, even third-generation Sino-Khmer reported difficulties when it came to literary language (with its high percentage of Pali) and Khmer writing. Sending Sino-Khmer children to Chinese schools was a practical necessity as well as a matter of cultural pride.

An ideal pattern was for children to attend Chinese school for several years—long enough to learn some Chinese and obtain a good foundation in math. After acquiring these skills, the child could be transferred to a public school. Many rural Sino-Khmer children, however, like those in my study, were not able to make the difficult transition to public school and dropped out, having completed only a few years in a Chinese school.[9]

For Sino-Khmer in the United States, the language groups continue to play an important economic role. Through the social networks these groups provide, businesspeople establish contacts later used to secure loans and form partnerships. These language groups are not formal associations. They have no regular or routine meetings. But members of the same group tend to socialize and participate in *tong-tiny* "rotating credit groups." Intermarriage within the group is also preferred, although it is not required in most parents' eyes. Nonetheless the degree of trust among those who share regional language background is quite remarkable. It is the willingness of Chinese Khmer to depend on such nonfamilial relationships to support economic endeavors that most clearly distinguishes Chinese business enterprises from those of ordinary Khmer.

One small restaurant owner whom I interviewed provides an unusually good illustration of this point. He had originally gone into business with a fellow Teochieu speaker, someone he knew only vaguely, but who had a significant amount of investment capital and was looking for a partner with experience as a cook. The wealthy Chinese supplied 70 percent of the capital for the restaurant; my interviewee had to put up only 30 percent, in addition to doing the cooking and other restaurant labor, with the help of his family. After about six months the wealthy partner decided he wanted out of the joint venture. The younger man lacked the capital with which to continue the business on his own and was frightened by the prospect of losing all that he and his family had invested. Faced with this desperate situation, he sought out other Chinese friends, all fellow Teochieu speakers, and asked to borrow various sums of money to buy his partner's share of the restaurant. He explained the results of his enquiries:

> I went to my friend who is now a high school teacher. He's a friend from thirty years ago from Chinese school in Cambodia. I quit school, but he continued on to public high school and then to college for one year. I just called him and said that I needed money for the restaurant. We didn't sign any papers. He didn't have much cash, but he had a credit card and I asked him to get me a loan of five thousand dollars on his credit card. I paid it off when I could with the interest to the company. My friend didn't ask for anything, no interest or payment for himself. I also borrowed a couple thousand from a couple of other friends. Those guys didn't want interest either; they just want to see the business do well. Most of them I helped sometime too. So we trust each other. When the business does well, I pay them what I can.

Stories like these of informal loan arrangements are extremely common among Sino-Khmer. So, too, is the pattern of joint ventures involving multiple partners and modest amounts of capital pooled by members of the same dialect group. In many such cases, the partners are not linked by ties of kinship, though they may have a history of longstanding, if diffuse, friendship. More remarkable, perhaps, is the pattern of contract through which such investments are made. No papers are signed, no formal interest is demanded, and there is no more severe mechanism of contract enforcement than the quality of the relationship and, more generally, one's reputation in the community. Similarly, as one grocery store owner explained to me, debt repayment is made in a flexible fashion, responsive to fluctuations in business: "My friend doesn't ask for anything, but I know that I have to pay some amount, like maybe one hundred dollars a month on a ten-thousand-dollar loan. And if the business is good, I pay them more, like maybe two hundred dollars. But it's not like the bank. They have so many rules and if business is slow and you don't pay the interest one month, they take your store. Friends are not like that. If you have a bad month, you just pay nothing."

The relationship here is by no means purely altruistic, as there is a very distinct expectation that loans will be repaid and, equally important, profits will be shared in a fashion that more or less reflects the proportion of capital each partner-friend has in the enterprise. Thus, when business is good, partners expect to receive a larger share of the profit, the proportion of which can in absolute terms represent significant interest on capital. Nonetheless, the basic difference between such informal contracts and ordinary bank loans is quite remarkable. If business is poor, partners do not demand payment. However, if things continue to go badly, partners can demand to be bought out.

Khmer Cultural Values and Economic Behavior

In contrast to the Sino-Khmer pattern described above, the consensus among most Cambodians, both ordinary and Sino-Khmer, is that ordinary Khmer are less single-minded in their dedication to business affairs and more reluctant to assume economic risks. The clearest example of this distinctive difference, one frequently remarked upon by Khmer and Sino-Khmer alike, is the tendency of ethnic Khmer who have acquired some savings to place the purchase of a home above the opening or expansion of a business. Sino-Khmer business owners were quite emphatic that they felt it wiser to defer the purchase of a home until their businesses were on firm financial ground. Conversely, several ordinary Khmer shop owners linked their financial difficulties to their home mortgage bills. One female grocery store owner explained how after paying her mortgage and utilities bills on her home and the rent and utilities on her store, she had no more capital to invest in new stock. She acknowledged that this had been a serious miscalculation on her part. And yet, though less single-minded in their commitment to business investment, non-Chinese Khmer are regarded as significantly more concerned with an array of nonbusiness social investments related to one's standing, or "face," in the community. This preoccupation is notably different from that of their more independent-minded Sino-Khmer counterparts. For ethnic Khmer a key feature of one's standing in the community is the ability to make generous contributions to the temple and to sponsor expensive religious and life-cycle ceremonies that serve to increase not only one's prestige in this life but also one's store of merit for the next.[10] In his detailed study of Theravada Buddhism in Southeast Asia, Robert Lester underscores this association between merit and social status among Khmer Buddhists: "In general, the more merit a man 'makes,' the greater is his social status. The power and prestige which one holds are the result of past merit-making; likewise, the maintenance and enhancement of status depend on continued merit-making." In this way many ordinary Khmer believe that, "one's merit potential is his social mobility potential" (Lester 1973, 147).

The difference between Khmer and Sino-Khmer social investments is related, in part, to the difference in religiousness. Although Sino-Khmer typically adopt Theravada Buddhism, for many it involves little more than a nominal involvement, with aspects of Chinese Buddhist religious practice and ancestor worship also maintained.[11] In virtually every Sino-Khmer business, for example, one observes a small Chinese altar with a statue of the Buddha, candles, incense, food offerings, and an inscription in Chinese characters on red paper. One young Sino-Khmer male explained the religious participation of Sino-Khmer in the following terms: Real Cambodians probably go to the temple more often than Chinese because the Chinese work too hard to go. "But I give food for temple celebrations if they come to my place to ask. I do that for the good feeling and because it is my tradition too . . . because I am Cambodian. As for beliefs like destiny, reincarnation, well, most Cambodians believe in that; Chinese, maybe only 1 percent believe and the rest believe in hard work. I don't believe that if you go to the temple you will have a long life or a better life. I go because it's part of my tradition."

Again, this contrast highlights what is perhaps the most fundamental difference between Sino-Khmer and ordinary Khmer. Ordinary Khmer expend significantly more time and energy, as well as surplus capital, on merit-making endeavors and status-generating activities. A preoccupation with issues of destiny, face, and reincarnation, as well as social standing within the community, results in a significantly different attitude toward business endeavors among non-Chinese Khmer.

For these ordinary Khmer, the idea of taking one's capital and risking it in a deferred and highly uncertain investment—especially uncertain given the widespread recognition that ordinary Khmer lack the entrepreneurial skills of their Sino-Khmer counterparts—strikes many as perilous at the very least. One Khmer widow whom I knew quite well confided that she had dreams of opening a small market someday. But she immediately added that she would never consider telling any of her friends or acquaintances about her aspirations. If she did tell them of her plans, she said, and then the store did not materialize, she would be called a liar (*kohoc*) and the community would judge her badly. When I asked how anyone can possibly make plans for the future if they are constantly afraid of losing face should their plans fail, she said, "You just don't dare talk about it until you are sure. You can only talk with your family and depend on your family for advice. Then, when you open the restaurant everyone is very surprised and they will say, 'she didn't say anything about that; that's a good lady.' " The cautious attitude displayed here in social relationships and the sharing of confidence as regards future projects is vividly captured in a well-known Khmer saying, "The less often you open your mouth, the fewer mistakes you make."

The concern for public opinion, the absence of mutual aid associations, and the lack of precedent for joint-venture enterprise make ordinary Khmer extremely hesitant to call on friends and associates for economic assistance. The result is that what economic partnerships there are are effectively limited to family relationships or, in rare cases, the few non-kin who, by virtue of long-standing social ties, have been elevated to the status of fictive kin. Khmer frequently say that they are too ashamed (*ien*) to ask their friends to loan them money. They express the fear that if they ask a friend for money and he refuses, the real problem is that the person is not really a friend but "looks down on you as if you are lower status." Whatever the case, the seriousness with which Khmer take their standing in the community makes it difficult to interpret such failed initiatives as anything other than a loss of face, which is to say, a loss of that which most Khmer regard as most integral to their social being.

Unassimilated Chinese who lived in Cambodia are themselves aware of this basic difference between Chinese and Khmer. One first-generation Chinese shop owner, raised in Cambodia, summed up the contrast with the rather dry observation that "Cambodians are less interested in money than in status because they believe that power is bigger than money. They say, 'if you have money with no power you can do nothing. If you have power you can make money easily.' " Of course, non-Chinese Khmer summarize the contrast differently, emphasizing that the Chinese may be economically savvy, but it is at the cost of being so thoroughly money-grubbing as to lack the cultural sensitivity required for dignified social standing. A similar contrast—between Chinese as hard-nosed and independent to the point of social disesteem and non-Chinese Southeast Asians as status- and power-conscious to the point of being economically inefficient—has been widely noted in other parts of Southeast Asia (cf. Jay 1969; Keeler 1986).

This contrast is again related to aspects of Cambodian history. In prewar Cambodia, power and high social standing were typically obtained through government employment. Although the majority of ordinary Khmer in the Boston area had been farmers in Cambodia, they were familiar with and, to a certain degree, endorsed the ideal of the Khmer middle class—to become or to have their children become a white collar functionary in government. According to this ideal, it was sufficient that a single individual, the head of the family, work to support his whole family. The wife, then, could devote her free time to religious and social activities; she might also open a small business on the side. In some cases, the father's bureaucratic position might even be used to finance quite extensive business arrangements, but these were viewed as subsidiary to the father's central bureaucratic role and status.[12]

Under the influence of their new homeland, Khmer notions of status and economic mobility are, of course, changing. As one interviewee aptly commented, "In Cambodia if you hold a government position you are set for life, but here, they always try to throw you out." Nonetheless, many Khmer in the United States still hold to a version of this middle-class, bureaucratic ideal. Rather than looking to government, however, upwardly mobile Khmer in the United States look toward the credentialed professions as the most appealing avenue for realizing a modified version of this ideal pattern—a strategy that has had only limited success among lower-class Khmer (Rumbaut and Ima 1988; Smith-Hefner 1990, 1993). In any case, the practical consequences of this modified ideal and other social constraints are quite real. Few Khmer regard independent business activity as an attractive or feasible option for upward movement into their new host society.

Emergent Patterns of Khmer Entrepreneurship

Though its actual dimensions are small, there are nonetheless several interesting aspects to business activity among non-Chinese Khmer in the Boston area. First and most notably, primary ownership of a good number of enterprises (especially hair and nail salons, but also small stores) lies in the hands of Khmer women, while their husbands, if there is a husband at all, play a secondary, supportive role. This matrifocal pattern in part reflects the traditional dominance of women in the domestic economy, as well as their predominant role in small-scale marketing (Ebihara 1968). It is perhaps remarkable that in Sino-Khmer families this same pattern obtains, in notable contrast to the patriarchal pattern of economic control in many Chinese families.

Second, even where ordinary Khmer engage in enterprise, there is an important difference in the way they invest their profits compared with most Sino-Khmer. Sino-Khmer tend to reinvest a greater proportion of their profits back into their business endeavors than do ordinary Khmer. Among Sino-Khmer, in particular, one finds a widespread pattern of economic expansion, in which a business owner slowly establishes several related business endeavors. For example, the Sino-Khmer owner of a successful photography business rents traditional and Western-style wedding clothing and jewelry to customers, as an option in the various photo service packages he offers for weddings. His business also rents Asian film videos (dubbed in Khmer) and offers videotaping services for special occasions. Most recently, he has added a courier service to Cambodia for the delivery of video messages, photos, small goods, letters, and money to friends and relatives left behind. The courier returns with handicraft items made in Cambodia, including fabrics, religious statues, carvings, and musical instruments, which are for sale in the shop. In some cases such expansions may become separate enterprises, which are then placed in the hands of different members of the owner's extended family. A Sino-Khmer video store owner, for example, opened a second shop for his younger brother when the youth graduated from high school. He has plans to open a third, he says, to be managed by a nephew who has recently arrived from the camps. By contrast with this pattern of Sino-Khmer business expansion, ordinary Khmer tend to invest a larger proportion of their profits in goods and endeavors that enhance their social capital within the community without directly enhancing their business capital. Such events include sponsorship of ritual festivals, the purchase of a new home, or travel to Cambodia to visit relatives. Though all these investments help to establish one's standing in the community, most are also expensive, not just of capital but of time and social energy as well. As Sino-Khmer business people readily observe, whatever their social benefits, such activities divert capital away from business enterprises and may undermine the long-term success of a business.

Whatever the salience of this contrast between Sino-Khmer and non-Chinese Khmer business people, my research among the two groups in the Boston area revealed that on one point they show an unexpectedly similar attitude. A large number of the small business owners I interviewed, Khmer and Sino-Khmer alike, volunteered the opinion that they would prefer to be doing something else other than running their own business. These individuals view their business enterprises as preferable to the other types of low-status employment available to them, but the great majority did not regard their businesses as satisfying ends in themselves. They complained of the long hours associated with their work (typically ten to twelve hours a day, seven days a week), and lamented the never-ending stress and uncertainty. Many said quite bluntly that their businesses had become an obstacle to a satisfying family and social life. One would suspect that, rather than reflecting the reproduction of premigration values here in the United States, this critical attitude toward business may be new, and strongly influenced by business owners' awareness that, here in the United States, there are avenues to social autonomy and economic success other than through business enterprise.

Few business owners, for example, said they expected or wanted their children to succeed them in their businesses. Most were quite deliberately encouraging their children to pursue credentialed professional positions in health care, computers, or engineering. They regarded these "soft" professions as more economically attractive, and less demanding of time and energy than ownership of a small business. Here again, one suspects, is a broadening of economic horizons that reflects quite clearly the changed employment opportunities in the United States. A commitment to business ideals remained, nonetheless. Though most business owners hoped their children would go into more comfortable professions, they quickly added that, should their children fail to obtain a degree or to secure professional employment, there would be a place for them in the family enterprise.

The patterns of business activity seen among Sino-Khmer are not surprising, given what is known about business activities among overseas Chinese in East and Southeast Asia. Gordon Redding (1990), for example, has described the way in which business among overseas Chinese is characterized by a predominance of family firms, in which parents and children are deeply and often obsessively involved in joint enterprise. Redding similarly emphasizes the way in which extra-family relationships of language, clan, and community provide important measures of trust and confidence in business interaction, all of which serve to facilitate Chinese business endeavors. What is surprising, perhaps, is the degree to which some of the key features associated with Chinese ethnicity have been diluted or weakened among many Sino-Khmer. Nonetheless, this assimilation process appears to have stopped short of diluting the distinctive economic advantage Chinese enjoy over ordinary Khmer.

Viewed from the perspective of non-Chinese Khmer, the pattern is perhaps a bit less familiar, but it is quite intelligible. Where ethnic Khmer sought upward mobility they turned to bureaucratic positions, not business. This pattern reinforced the Khmer cultural bias toward social and political standing rather than pure wealth as a determinant of status. The pattern was further reinforced by the force of ethnic rivalries between Khmer and Sino-Khmer, though, by Southeast Asian standards, these were moderate and rarely escalated to the extreme levels of open hostility seen elsewhere (Willmott 1967, 40). Through this process of ethnic differentiation, money-mindedness came to be regarded as a feature of Chinese identity, while ritual consumption and social largesse remained markers of Khmer ethnic identity.

In the United States, this basic pattern has been perpetuated, but with the additional twist that upwardly mobile Khmer here look not to government but to education and the professions as their vehicle for social advancement. Despite this ideal, most Khmer have not been particularly successful in obtaining professional positions in the United States, and many Khmer children are struggling in American schools (Rumbaut and Ima 1988; Smith-Hefner 1993). Nonetheless, it is interesting to note that those Khmer individuals who do succeed at upward mobility often move so thoroughly into a new social universe, an American one, that they end up far removed from the embedded social communities from which they or their parents might have come, and more thoroughly adopt the economic and cultural customs of their host country. In so doing, some of these successful Khmer end up so distant from the integral Khmer community that they disappear from its horizons entirely.

This, one suspects, may remain the pattern for some time to come: more and more successful Khmer assimilated into American culture. But if the experiences of Chinese and Japanese are any model, as this community of successful Khmer-Americans grows, it may rediscover and reinvent, albeit in a fashion that reflects their American circumstances, aspects of their ethnic culture. Such a process may have important implications for Khmer identity in the United States. However, it seems unlikely to transform the basic pattern of Khmer economic activity: the avoidance of risky enterprise in favor of expansive social investments and, for upwardly-mobile Khmer, higher education, through which one moves into the professions rather than business.

Notes

1. Although he does not provide comparative figures, Stephen Gold's study (1992) of Vietnamese immigrants in California indicates that Sino-Vietnamese predominate in entrepreneurial activities there too. Unlike the Khmer, however, a significant number of non-Chinese Vietnamese also engage in small- and even large-scale enterprise.

2. On differences between refugees and immigrants with regard to economic orientation see Bernard (1977), and Portes and Rumbaut (1990).

3. This initial research (1988–90) was supported by grants from the University of Massachusetts and the Spencer Foundation.

4. The Massachusetts Office of Refugees and Immigrants (MORI) estimates that there were twenty-five thousand to thirty thousand Khmer refugees living within the Greater Metropolitan Boston Area in 1988, the last year for which they provide separate figures on Khmer (MORI 1988). The numbers I cite here are an adjustment of MORI's figures based on current estimates by community leaders, public schools, and social service agencies. On Lowell's population see also Toula Vlahou's article in the *Lowell* (Massachusetts) *Sun*, 6 March 1988, and Tom Coakley's article in the *Boston Sunday Globe*, 22 January 1989.

5. Based on interviews with the heads of several Boston area Chinese social service agencies and an informal survey of the signs on Chinatown stores and restaurants, it seems that more than 75 percent of Boston's Chinatown establishments are actually now run by Sino-Vietnamese. Community leaders indicate that their transfer was facilitated by a shared language, Cantonese. (Most Sino-Khmer, by contrast, speak Teochieu.)

6. An exception is the differentiation made between Vietnamese and Sino-Vietnamese. Most studies of Southeast Asian refugees which make reference to "Chinese" are, in fact, referring to Vietnamese Chinese.

7. In the mid-1960s, anthropologist William Willmott (1967, 17) estimated the Chinese population in Cambodia to be 7.4 percent of the total.

8. For example, Gold (1994), in a study of Sino-Vietnamese entrepreneurs, mentions that many have changed their names from Vietnamese to Chinese to facilitate linkages with other Chinese entrepreneurs.

9. Chinese schools, as private enterprises, were more expensive than the public schools. They were also generally of lower quality (Whitmore 1985, 64–65).

10. See Charles Keyes (1983) for an interesting discussion of a similar pattern among Buddhist Thai.

11. Willmott (1967, 38–39), writing about the situation of Chinese in prewar Cambodia, states that religious behavior is "a clear index of ethnicity particularly with regard to participation in the support and activities of the temples."

12. Reports of those community members who have visited friends and family living in California or Washington, D.C. indicate that a similar pattern is being followed by at least some of the remaining Khmer elite who have obtained positions in government-supported refugee programs. A similar ideal apparently holds among middle-class Vietnamese as well (Gold 1992; Kibria 1989).

References

Bernard, William S. 1977. "Immigrants and Refugees: Their Similarities, Differences, and Needs." *International Migration* 14, no. 4: 267–81.

Bonacich, Edna. 1973. "A Theory of Middleman Minorities." *American Sociological Review* 38 (October): 583–94.

Boston Persistent Poverty Project. 1992. "Recognizing Poverty in Boston's Asian American Community." Boston: Boston Foundation.

Caplan, Nathan, John K. Whitmore, and Quang L. Bui. 1985. *South-East Asian Refugee Self-Sufficiency Study.* Ann Arbor, Mich.: Institute for Social Research.

Ebihara, May M. 1968. "A Khmer village in Cambodia." Ph.D. diss., Columbia University.

——. 1985. "Khmer." In *Refugees in the United States: A Reference Handbook,* edited by David W. Haines. Westport, Conn.: Greenwood Press.

Gold, Stephen J. 1992. *Refugee Communities: A Comparative Field Study.* Newbury Park, Calif.: Sage.

——. 1994. "Chinese-Vietnamese Entrepreneurs in California." In *New Asian Immigrants in Los Angeles and Global Restructuring,* edited by Paul Ong, Edna Bonacich and Lucie Cheng. Philadelphia: Temple University Press.

Hood, Marlowe, and David A. Ablin. 1987. "A Path to Cambodia's Present." In *The Cambodian Agony,* edited by David A. Ablin and Marlowe Hood. New York: M. E. Sharpe.

Jay, Robert T. 1969. *Javanese Villagers: Social Relations in Rural Modjokuto.* Cambridge: MIT Press.

Keeler, Ward W. 1986. *Javanese Shadow Plays: Javanese Selves.* Princeton: Princeton University Press.

Keyes, Charles F. 1983. "Economic Action and Buddhist Morality in a Thai Village." *Journal of Asian Studies* 42, no. 4: 851–68.

Kibria, Nazali. 1989. "Patterns of Vietnamese Refugee Women's Wagework in the U.S." *Ethnic Groups* 7: 297–323.

Lester, Robert C. 1973. *Theravada Buddhism in Southeast Asia.* Ann Arbor: University of Michigan Press.

MORI (Massachusetts Office for Refugees and Immigrants). 1988. *Refugees and Immigrants in Massachusetts: A Demographic Report.* Boston: Commonwealth of Massachusetts, Executive Office of Human Services.

Portes, Alejandro, and Ruben G. Rumbaut. 1990. *Immigrant America: A Portrait.* Berkeley: University of California Press.

Purcell, Victor. 1973. "Chinese Society in Southeast Asia." In *Southeast Asia: The*

Politics of National Integration, edited by John T. McAlister, Jr. New York: Random House.

Redding, S. Gordon. 1990. *The Spirit of Chinese Capitalism.* New York: Walter De Gruyter.

Rumbaut, Ruben G., and Kenji Ima. 1988. "The Adaptation of South-east Asian Refugee Youth: A Comparative Study." Final Report to the Office of Refugee Resettlement. San Diego: San Diego State University.

Smith-Hefner, Nancy. 1990. "Language and identity in the Education of Boston-Area Khmer." *Anthropology and Education Quarterly* 21, no. 3: 250–68.

——. 1993. "Education, Gender, and Generational Conflict among Khmer Refugees." *Anthropology and Education Quarterly* 24, no. 2: 137–58.

Vickery, Michael. 1984. *Cambodia: 1975–1982.* Boston: South End Press.

Whitmore, John K. 1985. Chinese from Southeast Asia. In *Refugees in the United States: A Reference Handbook.* Ed. David W. Haines. Westport, Conn.: Greenwood Press.

Willmott, William E. 1967. *The Chinese in Cambodia.* Vancouver: University of British Columbia.

Chapter 8

"Staying Close to Haitian Culture": Ethnic Enterprise in the Immigrant Community

Marilyn Halter

The decade of the 1980s saw a dramatic increase in the number of Haitian immigrants settling in the Boston metropolitan area, arrivals who came to take advantage of the then booming economy in the region. Twenty-five years ago fewer than three thousand Haitians lived in Greater Boston, and as one interviewee put it, "meeting another Haitian was a miracle." The current population has mushroomed to an estimated forty thousand to sixty thousand residents. The official 1990 census data show the total at fewer than twenty thousand, but it is widely acknowledged by both Haitian community leaders and the Haitian Consulate in Boston that this number represents a formidable undercount, largely because a majority in the Haitian community are undocumented. According to consulate officials, even the higher figure of sixty thousand is still too low an estimate of this steadily growing population. Some came to the city directly from their island homeland, but many more have relocated from other large Haitian-American communities such as New York City or Miami. Others have migrated south from Montreal, Canada.

With this influx came a proliferation of small business ventures, initiated primarily to serve the needs of coethnics. These new entrepreneurs have had to struggle against many odds. Although most left Haiti to escape political persecution, seeking asylum in the United States, the vast majority do not hold refugee status but are categorized as economic migrants. Thus, many arrive having experienced the violent disruptions and consequent disadvantages of political refugees, but cannot take advantage of the resettlement services that come with refugee status in the United States. Furthermore, as one of the newest populations to settle in the area, they do not benefit from an already established coethnic community from which they could derive support. Within the existing community, intragroup conflict is rife, the legacy of the politically unstable conditions of the Haitian society from which they came. Finally, they are a black immigrant population that faces racial discrimination once they arrive in this country.

Coming from a highly class-stratified society, Haitians must adjust to a situation in the United States where race predominates over both social class and ethnicity. Members of the first generation are more likely than later generations to exhibit a strong national identity, speak Haitian Creole, which is not simply a dialect of French but a language of its own, and associate primarily with coethnics. In general, they do not actively identify with African Americans, although the immigrant children are beginning to reverse this pattern. They are more willing to shed their traditional culture, speak English exclusively, and attempt to fit into black America. Haitians also view themselves as distinct from other Afro-Caribbean migrants. They shun identifying themselves as West Indians, because of the difference in language from their English-speaking Caribbean counterparts, because of their differing cultural background, and because of the Haitians' unique history of early self-rule. Faced with racial discrimination as well as significant levels of anti-immigrant bias, Haitian Americans have had to juggle a complex mix of social, cultural, regional, and racial identifications in the process of adapting to their new communities.

Thus far, they have not been able either to establish an economic niche for themselves or to expand their entrepreneurial activities beyond the compatriot community. Despite these conditions, the population continues to grow and get organized, with businesses playing an important role in this development. In conjunction with the community service sector and the many radio and television outlets in the area featuring Haitian programming, these enterprises become a critical site for social networking, political organizing and debate, information exchange, and the maintenance of Haitian cultural forms. The entrepreneurs, community leaders, and those involved in the Haitian media combine and overlap to form the nexus of the immigrant settlement in Boston.

Because of the growing numbers overall, the inflow of Haitian newcomers to the United States has become a more visible phenomenon. Widespread public attention in recent years has focused on the plight of refugees fleeing Haiti after the 1991 ouster of the democratically elected President Jean-Bertrand Aristide. What most people do not realize is that the migration of Haitians to this country actually dates back more than two hundred years when a small stream of colonists, free mulattoes, and slaves escaped the turmoil of insurrection brewing in their homeland, then called Santo Domingo. African slaves had been brought to the island in the eighteenth century by French colonists to work on sugar plantations. In no other society in history based on slave labor have the slaves initiated and carried out a successful revolution. They overthrew French rule in 1804 to become an independent nation, the second oldest republic in the New World. Refugees of the Haitian Revolution scattered along the U.S. coastal cities of New Orleans, Charleston, Philadelphia, and New York, and even as far north as Boston. Members of this early group of settlers hold the distinction in U.S. history of representing the first voluntary migration of people of African descent.

A second wave of Haitian migrants arrived in the first third of the twentieth century during the U.S. occupation of Haiti from 1915 to 1934, settling primarily in New York City. The current and largest outflow began in the late 1950s when Francois Duvalier became president of Haiti, inaugurating what would be a long and brutal regime. Followed by his son, Jean-Claude, together they ruled Haiti for thirty years until 1986. Initially, the migrants from this last wave were primarily intellectuals, professionals, and political refugees of the middle and elite classes attempting to escape the Duvaliers' reign of terror. But by the mid-1960s, all sectors of the society began seeking relief from the high unemployment, shrinking opportunities, and oppressive rule of this most impoverished country of the Western Hemisphere through mass outmigration. Dire political and economic circumstances in Haiti have made emigration a matter of life or death for many who have found myriad ways, both legal and clandestine, of reaching U.S. shores, including much-publicized, desperate attempts to make the eight-hundred-mile crossing in leaky and overcrowded boats. Many sold everything they owned to book passage to this country.[1]

More than half of those claiming Haitian ancestry in the United States reside in New York City and are dispersed throughout neighborhoods where African Americans and other Afro-Caribbeans also tend to live.

But within the Miami metropolitan area Haitian newcomers have created the beginnings of an ethnic economy, a section known as Little Haiti, and modeled after Miami's flourishing Little Havana. In the late 1970s and early 1980s, along with the more than sixty thousand Haitian "boat people" arriving in south Florida, a secondary migration of primarily middle-class Haitians who had originally settled in New York began to relocate to Miami as well. Operating on a much smaller scale and with more obstacles than its Cuban counterpart, Little Haiti has, nevertheless, grown to include a range of enterprises from ethnic microbusinesses to more established ventures selling Haitian and French-style products, a well-developed community service sector, venues for Haitian music and art, and a strong presence within the local educational system. When a new public school opened in the neighborhood, it was named Toussaint L'Ouverture Elementary after the Haitian revolutionary leader. Low-cost housing is available to residents of the enclave, an area that is situated close to the garment factories and warehouses in Miami where many of the immigrants are employed (Portes and Stepick 1993, 176–94).

The period of sustained economic growth in Massachusetts during the 1980s also triggered a shift in the Haitian population of the Northeast away from the established community in New York City, where many middle- and working-class families felt constrained by rising crime rates and residential congestion. They were drawn to the Boston area. Its reputation for good schools and its strong economy held out the promise of economic advancement for themselves and educational opportunity for their children. Like the Soviet Jewish refugees in the city, many Haitians saw the Boston community as a haven for intellectuals. But it was not only the most highly educated who were attracted to the region in those years. The influx included migrants from a wide range of socioeconomic and educational backgrounds seeking employment, especially in the region's growing service industries. Within Greater Boston, the Haitian newcomers have clustered primarily in the areas of Dorchester, Mattapan, Roxbury, Hyde Park, Cambridge, and Somerville, often settling in neighborhoods where other black residents, either African American or West Indian, are also concentrated. Some, who have become upwardly mobile, have moved out to suburban locations.

The Haitian community of Boston began to coalesce in the mid-1970s, marked by the political celebration of Haitian flag day in May 1974 with a boisterous procession of honking cars and much waving of the anti-Duvalier blue-and-red flags. The first Haitian bands, a dance club, and a cultural center were also formed at that time, along with a sprinkling of new businesses. By the early 1980s, both the Cambridge Haitian American Association (CHAMA) and the Haitian Multi-Service Center in Dorchester had opened their doors, offering a range of programs including employment, housing and legal assistance, educational counseling, Creole and English classes, document translation, and other interpreting services. New nonprofit organizations continue to spring up, but CHAMA and the Haitian Multi-Service Center remain the most significant.

Religious participation is high among the newcomers. Although most Haitians are Roman Catholic, increasing numbers are joining evangelical Protestant congregations, a legacy of the Protestantism brought to Haiti by hundreds of American missionaries. Most of the immigrant Protestant worshipers are of the Baptist denomination. Currently, there are some forty churches in the Greater Boston area serving the Haitian community, with most offering services in Creole and some in French. Haitian pastors are taking greater leadership roles in their own congregations and in interchurch affairs. Many Haitian immigrants have creatively combined their more institutionalized Christian practices with less formal, traditional vodun religious beliefs. A growing number of families send their children to parochial schools.

One of the defining features of the Greater Boston Haitian community is the extended network of approximately thirty radio and television outlets that broadcast Haitian programming, usually in Creole. Haitian music and news from the homeland are broadcast throughout the day. Educational, cultural, and religious programs are offered on both the radio and local cable stations. Although the various programs come and go, changing names and owners, merging and dividing, the range of these media sources and the importance placed on them are unique to the Haitian immigrant community.

Typically, Haitian émigrés remain close to their relatives in Haiti. Family members already in the United States help the others to come in classic chain migration fashion. Although no statistics are available on the subject, it is widely understood that the money sent by Haitians from this country to their families and relatives in Haiti is one of their most important sources of revenue. When travel is not risky, Haitian immigrants who can afford it often visit Haiti. For the children of the wealthy in Haiti, trips to the United States, particularly Miami, are more frequent than travel from the capital city of Port-au-Prince to another part of the country, particularly with the recent political turmoil. It has also become more common for wealthy Haitian parents to send their children to U.S. schools, and English and French bilingual schools in Haiti have become increasingly popular. Hence, at many levels, the back and forth movement and interpenetration of Haitian and American cultures permeates the Haitian-American immigrant experience.

Portrait of the Haitian Entrepreneur

For this study, twenty-nine in-depth, open-ended interviews were conducted, twenty-two with Haitian immigrant business owners and seven with Haitian community leaders. The participants were contacted through snowball sampling.[2] Their occupations before migration varied widely, from employment in accounting, marketing, or clerical jobs to work as radio announcers, laboratory technicians, mechanics, engineers, and teachers. A handful had been self-employed in Haiti and eight of those interviewed had at least one parent who had owned a business there, including selling cloth, renting trucks, lending money, and managing small grocery stores. Because the job market has been extremely tight, the majority tried to survive in Haiti's informal sector. Overall the level of education among the owners was above that of the average Haitian immigrant. The great majority had attended high school; six had a college education or more. Some had taken additional adult education classes. Like much of the middle-class Haitian immigrant population at large, most of the entrepreneurs reported visiting Haiti regularly.

Businesses represented in the Greater Boston area included food and clothing stores, restaurants and bakeries, day care centers, beauty salons and supplies, transportation (car rental, taxis), printing, record stores, and agencies providing one or several of the following services: translation, money transfer, insurance, real estate, accounting, and travel. Most of the enterprises were recently established. On average, immigrants opened their businesses about ten years after arriving in the United States.

The establishments are small-scale, usually opened with the owner's savings and sometimes just breaking even or yielding very small benefits. About half of the self-employed also held down another full- or part-time job to make ends meet. These arrangements are usually perceived as a temporary solution to financial difficulties. Most hope to fully dedi-

166

cate themselves to their enterprises after a few years. Men predominate in entrepreneurship among the Haitian immigrant community. It was necessary to track down the sample of six women proprietors included in this study. Four of the six were divorced, whereas all but two of the male owners were married. All of the women were owners of traditional female operations.

Two primary reasons were given by the entrepreneurs as motivations for opening a business: the desire to improve one's status within the community and the need to be financially independent. Of lesser significance was discrimination in the job market. One important incentive to opening their own businesses is the prestige associated with owning or leading any kind of organization within the Haitian community. Most interviewees seemed more concerned about how they were perceived by their compatriots than by the American public. Entrepreneurship enables them to offer jobs to other Haitians, which carries additional clout. Having a business is a symbol of independence as well. Within the paternalistic system in Haiti, most large enterprises belong to rich families, and employees are underpaid and often not treated with respect. Thus, most of the population grew up resenting working for others and place a high value on personal autonomy. As one Haitian grocer put it, "if you do not have your own business, you are not yet an adult."

All the entrepreneurs expressed great interest in their children's education, with some viewing the business as a guarantee that their offspring would receive a good education. Like most of the other immigrant groups, they generally did not envision involving their children permanently in their business ventures. Their hopes were pinned instead on enabling their sons and daughters to become professionals. Another frequent goal was to be able to return to Haiti and open a similar enterprise on the island.

Characteristics of Haitian Businesses

The great majority of the Haitian businesses employ no more than two people. In several cases, members of the family are the only ones to help out. Even when employees are not immediate family members, the business often functions like a family enterprise, with close friends or children of relatives working on a part-time basis and with informal arrangements related to scheduling, duties, and payment. Because the owners usually have personal ties with their workers, distinctions between the two are often blurred. In one case, an employee was actually trying to start up his own business on the premises. Arrangements where employees become partners or buy shares in the venture are not unusual. Most of the owners rely on their own limited knowledge of accounting to keep records; those using accountants or consultants are the rare exceptions.

The informality of employer-employee relations extends to the overall operation of many of the enterprises. Pricing policies as well as business hours are often irregular. The lack of standardized prices is a throwback to business procedures in Haiti when it was not unusual for an owner to decide how much to charge clients depending on how wealthy they looked. The practice of bargaining in the open market in Haiti has been replicated inside some established stores. The sometimes informal nature of scheduling in Haitian immigrant businesses is illustrated in the following excerpt from an interview with a relatively new owner:

> When do you open in the morning?
>> I open every day.
> From what time to what time do you open?
>> Sometimes, seven, seven thirty, eight.
> You don't have a regular opening time?
>> I'm supposed to open at six, but I haven't had the opportunity to open at six.
> At around what time do you close?
>> I close at around ten, ten thirty.
> When you advertised on the radio, was an opening and a closing time mentioned?
>> I gave the time I had planned to open . . . six o'clock. It is one of the reasons why I have stopped advertising. I want to be more confident about the time I should open and the time I should close.

Adding to the unreliability of scheduled hours of operation, some shops do not have telephones.

Haitian restaurants in the Boston metropolitan area often have a similar haphazard organization, with many listed menu items unavailable. Orders are sometimes confused or forgotten, and patrons may find that they are served something other than what they selected. In one restaurant, the waiters were so engrossed in the latest news report from Haiti being broadcast on the kitchen radio, that the customers had to make a determined effort to get the bill. Typically these ventures do not take credit cards. But along with this disorganization come generous portions, a relaxed atmosphere, and leisurely pacing that serve to replicate well the best in homestyle eating.

For the most part, customers are Haitian, with the balance composed of other blacks, particularly West Indians. Most shops cater to their Haitian compatriots, stocking their shelves with small quantities of ethnic products such as yams, plantains, yucca, and tropical-flavored fruit drinks. They also offer services that appeal to the needs of the immigrant community, such as money transfers and ethnic beauty care. These entrepreneurial efforts often bring only a slim margin of profit because of competition from supermarket chains, shopping malls, and other local ethnic businesses, such as Latino bodegas that carry similar items.

Many of these marginal operations survive by providing goods and services, both legal and illegal, other than those advertised. A record store may also sell popular Haitian snacks and drinks; a restaurant without a liquor license may offer Haitian rum. For some of the Haitian proprietors, the real money-making activity is in the illegal sale of *bolet* tickets, a form of lottery very popular in Haiti, where *bolet* banks are as visible as any small grocery store. The following interaction occurred at a shoe repair owned by a Haitian immigrant. As the shoemaker was fixing a broken buckle, the customer asked him, "Don't you have any shoes to sell?" The shoemaker replied, "What shoes are you talking about? What kind of shoes am I going to make? Where will I find money to make shoes? . . . Stop joking, don't you need a *bolet* number. Let me get it for you." In many of these ventures, one customer brings another and a relationship of trust develops between the clientele and the owner. Proprietors can then depend on their patrons not to denounce their illegal activities.

The businesses manage to survive in spite of the irregularities partly because they stay so small and localized, dependent on personal, trusting relationships with their clients. They are simply too insignificant for the justice system to bother to investigate. Because remaining a borderline, small-scale operation is a prerequisite for survival, business expansion is precluded. Most businesses also lack the financial stability to concentrate on broadening their enterprises to appeal to a wider clientele and, thus, are confined to a level of penny entrepreneurship.

Social Role of the Small Business

Most of what can be bought in the typical Haitian convenience store can also be found in the larger supermarkets or in smaller shops that hold regular hours and have consistent prices. So why would people frequent these more marginal enterprises, which usually also have greater diffi-culty in keeping their prices low? As one of the Haitian immigrant com-munity leaders put it, "it's as close as they can get to the Haitian culture." In some of these businesses, he continued, "no matter at what time you go, the same people are there. . . . It's almost a political club." Some of the barber shops are particularly known within the community for their political debates, one of the favorite conversational pastimes of Haitian men. "When you get there every man is speaking. They all feel entitled to express themselves. Informed or not, they talk," declared another inter-viewee. A third respondent, sketching the dynamics of a Haitian record store, stated that, "More political meetings are held there than in any political organization. Everybody meets there to discuss everything." He then told of the following incident to underscore his point: "The other day I went to a Haitian hairdresser. Do you understand? I wanted to have my hair cut. It was very crowded. I asked how long I would have to wait. They told me I may sit on the chair right away. None of the other people there needed to have their hair done! They had just gathered to hang out."

Another described a very popular business with no sign at its en-trance. There, customers can eat, have their hair cut, join a card game, or play dominoes. "It's like an undercover social club." Jeff Kantrowitz's coverage of Haitian immigrants in the *Boston Sunday Globe,* 24 October 1993, provided this illustration of the social role of small business in the community:

> At the New Yorker Department Store one recent weekend afternoon, counter clerk Joseph Paul, customer Eddy Jean and four fellow Haitians gathered around a television and milled among the racks of clothing in clear plastic sleeves. "Everyday we are assembled here," said Jean, ges-turing across the makeshift living room with one hand and clutching a Haitian-flag key chain with the other. "We live as a family. We talk about the problems of our country. We can't do anything, but we talk anyway."
>
> Any purchases? "There's not one person who buys anything here," said Jean. He held up an empty bottle of Veryfine fruit punch. "Me only, I buy this." A few days later, Joseph Paul had logged $13.40 in sales by 4:35 p.m.

None of the proprietors expressed any resentment at all toward the cus-tomers who congregate at their stores to socialize rather than spend money there. On the contrary, they tend to view their presence as some-thing quite positive. As one entrepreneur put it: "When I open a business for the community, I serve the community. . . . When you have a place to hang around in the community, it's where people are supposed to come to unwind. Sometimes even if the person doesn't come to buy, [that person] comes for ten to fifteen minutes to unwind. So it's a necessity. It is a service that you are offering to the community. That's enough."

The interviews revealed that the highest priority on the shopkeepers' list of keys to success was courtesy, which ranked even above education. In Haiti, the tradition of good neighbors is very much encouraged, and people are taught to treat each other with polite respect in family and village interactions. Thus, the Haitian entrepreneur values friendliness and courtesy above more competitive or aggressive behaviors, and there is no expectation that customers will make a purchase. One businessman spoke of the difference between the Haitian and the non-Haitian clientele. The non-Haitian shopper just comes to buy something and leaves, whereas the Haitian customer is very attentive to the way he or she is treated. Haitian entrepreneurs expect to appeal to coethnic patrons by receiving them well and maintaining an atmosphere that will draw them into the store and encourage them to stay. These decisions are quite detached from the demands of the market, and more often than not the social function of the enterprise supersedes economic considerations.

As a result, the businesses become a support service for the clientele. In some instances, strategic information may be exchanged that could help customers find a job, get medical assistance, or procure housing. The support networks created within these enterprises often play an important role in helping newcomers adjust to life in the United States, while enabling them to maintain elements of the Haitian culture, especially the Creole language, through their interactions with compatriots. In this way the ethnic economy serves to perpetuate the ethnic culture.

When customers do make purchases, knowing with whom they are interacting often becomes the deciding factor. A man from a small town in Haiti, who has a money transferring business, has a large clientele based on customers from the same village. Patrons may manifest their gratitude at being treated well by proprietors with purposeful expressions of loyalty. The owner of a hair salon whose premises had been destroyed by a fire described the response of her devoted customers: "When the building went on fire, they called me at my house. They told me you don't need to worry. You won't lose your clients. We are going to come, even if it has to be in your bathroom, we are going to come. We have to help you to get on your feet again. You understand? . . . They all came and I did not lose my clients."

Haitian Businesses and the Media

In addition to providing space for social interactions, some of the entrepreneurs help organize community entertainment, such as dances, concerts, fashion shows, and beauty contests, or political events, such as marches, rallies, and speakers. They sometimes sponsor these activities with the hope that it will increase their visibility and prestige. Owners keep in touch with the Haitian community via the well-developed media networks, and most of the larger businesses advertise on coethnic radio stations. In this way, the entrepreneurs support Haitian radio and television programming while, at the same time, benefiting from the media exposure. One owner reported being contacted by a radio station asking her to please advertise because the station was in need of support. The radio stations themselves, as with most of the other businesses, yield minimal returns, but they help owners achieve visibility and popularity.

The eagerness to get involved in the media stems from the immense political and educational role that the transistor radio has played in Haiti during the past twenty-five years. Without it, elections would not have been possible. Before its extensive use in Haiti, many of the population were not even aware of the existence of their country's president. The Haitian émigré community perpetuates radio's traditional role. In addition to providing news from Haiti, radio stations often broadcast interviews with Haitian intellectuals and professionals. In almost every instance, irrespective of the type of enterprise, Haitian radio or television programming provides the backdrop on the premises. Furthermore, copies of Haitian newspapers, especially the weekly *Haiti en Marche*, are readily available. Customers pore over the papers, usually while engaged in animated conversation about the latest news. On several occasions, the entrance to a Haitian grocery store was obstructed by a group of men watching a current event videotaped in Haiti.

Similarly, nonprofit Haitian organizations use radio and television outlets, particularly for educational programming directed at the Haitian community. Individuals involved in community service rely on ethnic businesses to publicize their activities, posting fliers or placing informational pamphlets in Haitian establishments. In one case, the director of a Haitian nonprofit organization was the owner of a transportation service, as well as a featured speaker on a radio program. The business sector works very closely with the nonprofit service providers and the Haitian communications network, playing a key integrative role in mobilizing the ethnic community and ensuring that the immigrants "stay as close as they can to Haitian culture."

Notes

1. For further background on the history of Haitian immigration to the United States, see Laguerre (1984).

2. Carolin Hudicourt provided invaluable research assistance in conducting and transcribing most of the interviews with Haitian business owners. All but three of the interviews were conducted in Haitian Creole. We spoke English in those sessions because either the interviewee preferred it or because it was felt that the social prejudices against Creole, considered to be a "primitive" language by some, could have created some discomfort. Furthermore, conducting the interview in French could have affected the interaction because mastery of the French language in Haiti is used as a measure of one's level of education and is also supposed to be indicative of socioeconomic background. It is, therefore, degrading to make mistakes in French. Communicating in flawless French is more important for some Haitians than communicating effectively.

References

Fontaine, Pierre-Michel. 1976. "Haitian Immigrants in Boston: A Commentary." In *Caribbean Immigration to the United States,* edited by Roy Bryce-Laporte and Delores M. Mortimer. Washington, D.C. Research Institute on Immigration and Ethnic Studies, Smithsonian Institution.

Kasinitz, Philip. 1992. *Caribbean New York: Black Immigrants and the Politics of Race.* Ithaca: Cornell University Press.

Laguerre, Michel. 1984. *American Odyssey: Haitians in New York City.* Ithaca: Cornell University Press.

Lawless, Robert. 1986. "Haitian Migrants and Haitian-Americans: From Invisibility into the Spotlight." *Journal of Ethnic Studies* 14: 29–70.

Lopescher, Gilburt, and John Scanlan. 1984. "Human Rights, U.S. Foreign Policy, and Haitian Refugees." *Journal of Interamerican Studies and World Affairs* 26, no. 3: 313–56.

Mittelberg, David, and Mary Waters. 1988. "The Process of Ethnogenesis among Haitian and Israeli Immigrants in the United States." *Ethnic and Racial Studies* 15, no. 3: 412–35.

Portes, Alejandro, and Alex Stepick. 1993. *City on the Edge: The Transformation of Miami.* Berkeley: University of California.

Stafford, Susan Buchanan. 1987. "The Haitians: The Cultural Meaning of Race and Ethnicity." In *New Immigrants in New York,* edited by Nancy Foner. New York: Columbia University Press.

Woldemikael, Tekle. 1989. *Becoming Black American: Haitians and American Institutions in Evanston, Illinois.* New York: AMS Press.

Contributors

MEHDI BOZORGMEHR is assistant professor of sociology at the City College, City University of New York. He is coprincipal investigator of "Ethnic Los Angeles," funded by the Russell Sage and Mellon Foundations, and "Immigrant and Native Engineers in California," funded by the Sloan Foundation. He has published many articles and book chapters on immigration, ethnicity, and entrepreneurship.

CLAUDIA DER-MARTIROSIAN is a doctoral candidate in sociology at UCLA, where she is writing a dissertation on the occupational achievement of Iranian immigrants in Los Angeles. She is the principal data analyst for Passport to Health projects at UCLA.

STEVEN J. GOLD, associate professor of sociology at Michigan State University, has published articles on immigration, ethnic communities, and visual sociology in *International Migration Review, Ethnic and Racial Studies, Research in Community Sociology, Society, Journal of Contemporary Ethnography, Asian and Pacific Migration Journal, Visual Sociology,* and several edited volumes. The past president of the International Visual Sociology Association, Gold is the author of *Refugee Communities: A Comparative Field Study* (1992) and is currently involved in a study of Israeli immigrants in Los Angeles.

MARILYN HALTER is a research associate at the Institute for the Study of Economic Culture, Boston University, where she is also an assistant professor of history and a member of the faculty of the American and New England Studies Program. She is the author of *The Historical Dictionary of the Republic of Cape Verde* (1988, with Richard Lobban) and *Between Race and Ethnicity: Cape Verdean American Immigrants, 1860–1965* (1993). Senior consultant for the "Race, Ethnicity, and Identity" section of the forthcoming *Encyclopedia of New England Culture,* she is also completing a book on the marketing of ethnicity in the United States.

• Contributors •

VIOLET JOHNSON is an assistant professor of history at Agnes Scott College, Decatur, Georgia. Before emigrating to the United States in 1985, she taught American history at Fourah Bay College in her native country of Sierra Leone. She received her Ph.D. from Boston College in 1992 and is currently revising her dissertation, "The Migration of British West Indian Immigrants in Boston, 1915–1950," for publication.

PEGGY LEVITT is an assistant professor of sociology at Harvard University. Her Ph.D. is from the Department of Urban Studies and Planning at the Massachusetts Institute of Technology where she has written a dissertation on the transnationalization of civil and political development.

IVAN LIGHT, professor of sociology at the University of California, Los Angeles, is the author of *Ethnic Enterprise in America* (1972), *Cities in World Perspective* (1983), *Immigrant Entrepreneurs: Koreans in Los Angeles, 1965–1982* (1988, with Edna Bonacich), and the editor of *Comparative Immigration and Entrepreneurship* (1993, with Parminder Bhachu). His forthcoming book is *Urban Entrepreneurs in America.*

CAESAR MAVRATSAS is a lecturer in sociology at the University of Cyprus. He received his Ph.D. in sociology from Boston University, where he was also a graduate fellow at the Institute for the Study of Economic Culture. His current work in progress involves a study of the effects of the Turkish invasion of 1974 on Greek-Cypriot economic culture and a comparative analysis of the meaning and implications of Hellenism in different parts of the world.

GEORGES SABAGH is director of the Center for Near Eastern Studies and professor emeritus of sociology at UCLA. He is launching a collaborative project on Ethnic Identity in Comparative Perspective: Armenians in Los Angeles, Moscow, and Yerevan. He has published more than seventy journal articles on a wide range of topics including fertility, residential mobility, and immigration in the United States, as well as, sociology and demography of the Middle East.

NANCY J. SMITH-HEFNER is an associate professor at the University of Massachusetts Boston, where she teaches in the graduate program in Bilingual/ English as a Second Language Studies. She has published numerous articles on Southeast Asian sociolinguistics and on various aspects of the Khmer refugee experience. She is currently completing work on a book that chronicles the efforts of Khmer-Americans to re-create family and community in the United States.

176

Index

West Indian enterprises (*continued*)
66; poverty among, 14, 16, 76; rotating
credit associations of, 12, 65–66, 70, 71;
in service sector, 14, 16, 61, 73–76. *See
also* West Indian enterprises
Willmott, William E., 147, 148
Wilson, Kenneth L., 27, 29–30, 39n. 3

women, 34, 51–53, 66; as business owners, 12, 51–52, 68, 75, 155, 167; role of,
in family enterprises, 11–12, 52, 102; as
wage workers, 34, 53, 75
Wong, Bernard, 33

Zhou, Min, 24, 31, 34